DIANA

HER
LIFE IN
FASHION

DIANA

HER LIFE IN FASHION

GEORGINA HOWELL

PAVILION

First published in Great Britain in 1998 by
PAVILION BOOKS LIMITED
London House, Great Eastern Wharf, Parkgate Road, London SW11 4NQ

Designed by Bridgewater Book Company

A CIP catalogue record for this book is available from the British Library

1 86205 147 X

Set in 10$^{1}/_{2}$ pt Bembo

Colour reproduction by DP Graphics
Printed and bound in Great Britain by Butler & Tanner, Frome and London
2 4 6 8 10 9 7 5 3 1

This book may be ordered by post direct from the publisher.
Please contact the Marketing Department. But try your bookshop first

'We give thanks for the life of a woman I am so proud to be able to call my sister, the unique, the complex, the irreplaceable Diana, whose beauty, both internal and external, will never be extinguished from our minds.'

FROM THE TRIBUTE BY EARL SPENCER
AT THE FUNERAL OF DIANA, PRINCESS OF WALES.

Contents

Acknowledgements

My grateful thanks go to the following:

The designers, who kindly cast back their memories, opened their archives and made the book a pleasure for me to research.

Mrs Shand Kydd, on behalf of the Princess' family, for her help and advice.

Meredith Etherington-Smith and Consuela Moorsom of Christie's, for their help throughout.

Colin Webb and Vivien James of Pavilion, who always saw this project as more than a coffee table picture book.

Emma Tait, whose good memory and long fascination with Diana made her an excellent database, as well as meticulous editor.

Clare Johnson, who tirelessly fitted the pieces together.

Robin Morgan, Editor of *The Sunday Times Magazine*, for his encouragement.

Introduction

'Whenever the Princess discussed her clothes with me,' says one of her favourite fashion designers, Jasper Conran, 'part of it was always: "What message will I be giving out if I wear this?" For her, that became the real language of clothes.'

Isolated as Diana was, she established a mode of continuous and tantalizing contact with the rest of the world. Through the barrage of her image, in print and on screen, the most famous woman in the world was able to express and edit the story of her life for a world-wide audience, and without a language barrier.

She enjoyed, and suffered, a singular equation. Every public appearance was immediately projected around the world to the biggest audience any star has ever had. Added to this was her genius for performance. Using the vocabulary of fashion, her changing but always radiant appearance, her expression and her body language, the Princess was able to act out the heartfelt phases and turning points of the sixteen difficult years that followed her wedding.

At the beginning, the signals were confused but she worked at herself, studying press clippings with fervent, and frequently misunderstood, application. It wasn't for vanity's sake that she spent hours studying her pictures and headlines, it was because she was learning to transmit her emotions and

previous page Four months before publication of *Diana: Her True Story*, the Princess signals her lonely state. On the Wales' official tour of India, in February 1992, she chose to be photographed conspicuously alone at the Taj Mahal, the famous monument to love. She wears a Catherine Walker suit in fuschia colours, already seen at Ascot and in Hong Kong.

left Snowdon's portrait of Diana for her twenty-first birthday, 1 July 1982, shows her earliest transformation from 'Shy Di' to a woman who loves the lens.

intentions through self-presentation, focusing always on the message she wished to communicate. At first, we received these signals almost subliminally. Latterly, when we knew the importance of the hand she was playing, we looked for them.

In 1993, after Diana had announced her withdrawal from public life, she happened to meet the actor Jeremy Irons. He told her, 'I'm having a year away from acting.' She responded with a smile, 'So am I!' But for the camera and in public she was far more than an actor; without exaggeration, she became one of the best communicators of the twentieth century. The proof was there in the unprecedented trauma of grief that hit Britain and the rest of the world on the day we learned of her death.

Officially, Diana was voiceless and powerless, monitored by protection officers, followed by photographers and always under the watchful eyes of the royal family. In spite of these restraints, or maybe because of them, she learned to be a consummate operator of the media. She found a way to impart just those aspects of herself, or her life, she wanted to reveal at the time, so that almost always we perceived her as she wished to be seen.

If you could read between the lines, she told you of her problems through her few charity speeches, centred as they were on her work for those organizations. When she decided to reveal the whole story of her lonely marriage she did it by the back door, through a third-party link to the author of what would become a record-breaking best seller. Only once, two years before her death, did she answer direct questions in a television interview, recorded in secrecy. By then, she had become truly independent and had begun, reluctantly, to see that divorce was inevitable. During the course of her public life, she mentioned the predicaments of her sad personal life to many people, one to one; but to qualify for such confidences you had to be an intimate friend or relation, or one of the seriously ill or disabled people she met through her charity work.

Looking back on her vivid, touching life we may wonder why it was so important to her to make that contact, ensuring that we all understood the extraordinary Diana and Charles story from her point of view. Early clues lay in her childhood, but it was far more complex than that and there were many reasons. It was because her father was disappointed that she was not born a boy, the heir he wanted and needed; because her mother left home when she was six; because the man she adored and married didn't adore her in return; because the royal family made no attempt to understand her but instead manipulated her and then froze her out; because she was isolated from support and affection; because, more than anything, she feared that she would be blamed for the breakdown of her marriage and lose her sons. She had set out with dedication to be a good wife, she had supplied 'the heir and the spare' and then she had proved herself to be a popular and deeply caring Queen-in-the making. It was not to be. She ached to be 'Queen of Hearts' because her sterling efforts and qualities deserved to be recognized and she deserved to be loved.

Betrayed by the men she had loved, she trusted few people, and prized loyalty beyond any other virtue. Beyond Harry and William, there were a few friends and close relations who remained loyal, and there was her 'rock', her butler Paul Burrell. She came to believe there was no one else she could trust absolutely. The dutiful track record, the stardom and the showmanship all came out of that insecurity. Each perfectly groomed, graceful performance was an appeal: 'Love me'. And we did.

With hindsight, we can recognize how extraordinarily clear was Diana's presentation of herself as she endeavoured to help us understand and sympathize with her. Dress by dress, look by look, phase by phase, she illustrated for us the story of her life and her historic place in the decline of the image of the royal house of Windsor.

As the overwhelmed ingenue after her engagement in 1981, Diana's message was one of aspiration: 'I am a grown-up princess'. As she struggled to find her feet after the wedding, she adjusted to a demure and decorative

below This dress, worn in 1985, shows Diana's slightly daring side with its lace inset front and back. Diana set it off with her sapphire and diamond choker and earrings, a wedding gift from the Crown Prince of Saudi Arabia.

phase: 'I am a good wife and mother'. She tried so hard that it almost amounted to defiance: 'You *must* appreciate me'. As Charles continued to ignore his wife and seek the company of his mistress, Camilla Parker-Bowles, the royals and the public fell briefly under the spell of the boisterous Sarah Ferguson, who married Prince Andrew in 1986. Swept along in her sister-in-law's wake, a rebellious Diana was signalling 'I won't be effaced' as she dressed and conducted herself in public in ways she subsequently regretted.

The nineties brought a transformation. As a result of her triumphs on several foreign tours, a poised Diana, dressed for diplomacy, gained visibly in confidence: 'Now I can do it better than he can'. Around the time of the publication of Andrew Morton's book and the official separation six months later, she dressed for sympathy: 'Now you understand'. She then moved upbeat towards total independence. The message 'I am not a victim any more' was sharpened with a touch of vengeance: 'Look what he has lost'.

Diana's new hold on her mass audience was rooted in a potent combination of movie-star glamour and a genuine compassion for the sick and disabled. Her appearance during these years perfectly expressed either, or both, of these elements as appropriate. As she reached her final stage of metamorphosis she became something more than an idol, an icon. Jewels and fabulous clothing could no longer add anything to her mystique or status. On 25 June 1997, she symbolically jettisoned her wardrobe of state, selling her weighty embroidered satins, jewelled velvets and sequinned laces in seventy-nine lots at Christie's New York. To paraphrase Earl Spencer's address at her funeral, she needed no grand toilette to continue to generate her particular brand of magic. Ballgowns, tiaras and HRH discarded, she remained in any company the focus of all attention. Wherever she went, in simple shift dresses with little make-up, she lit the room. She had gone full circle, back to the kind of clothes that are available to all of us. The pictures of Diana that we remember most clearly from that last year were of her visit to the landmines of Angola in January. Under a face shield and protective waistcoat, she wore a white cotton shirt and chinos with flat moccasins.

We believe that she was on the brink of a new era when she died – but not the generally expected one of a second marriage. In the last significant press photographs, taken on holiday on the Fayed yacht just a few months after her Angola visit, she wore only a swimsuit. A numinous, solitary figure, she balanced at the extreme end of a diving board above the blue void. Her last message was almost certainly: 'I am free'.

below In Diana's last few years dressing down became as important as dressing up. She wanted the press to write about her work, not about her clothes. In Angola, she rolled up her sleeves and got down to work to highlight the landmines issue in plain white shirt and Armani jeans.

opposite In this official portrait by Snowdon, taken in 1991, Diana has chosen to wear the Spencer family tiara rather than the diamond and pearl tiara given to her by the Queen as a wedding gift. The Princess' somewhat stiff pose and the prominence of her sapphire engagement ring seems to convey simultaneously her central position in the royal family, and her separateness from it. The royal purple velvet dress, unusually low-cut for an official photograph, was by Victor Edelstein.

left Diana at her best and most relaxed: photographed with William and Harry for her Christmas card, 1994, in the plainest of white shirts and black trousers.

Raw Material

I t wasn't just that Diana needed a trousseau. On the day of her engagement, she had only one long dress, one silk shirt, one smart pair of shoes and a £30,000 sapphire-and-diamond engagement ring.

This hadn't mattered until now, because Lady Diana Spencer shared a flat, and an interchangeable wardrobe, in the Old Brompton Road with three girls who had similar tastes to her own. These friends were Carolyn Pride, who had been a contemporary at Westheath School and hunted with the East Kent, the Berkeley Square secretary Anne Bolton, and Virginia Pitman, who was taking a china-mending course. They pooled their V-neck lambswool sweaters, floral-patterned cotton skirts, frilly shirts with bows at the neck, Peruvian sweaters, padded waistcoats and Barbours. The only things they did not share were the silver lockets containing snaps of parents and family dogs, their Gucci bags and the pearl necklaces they tucked inside their Shetlands.

Offspring of the British middle-class establishment, they belonged to the style type christened 'Sloane Rangers' by journalists Ann Barr and Peter York – a reference to the area around Sloane Street in west London where these young people lived and worked. As a true blue aristocrat, Diana was a little different. She had cleaned and nannied for young married Sloanes, and had coined her own name for them: the 'velvet hairbands'.

Then, on 17 September 1980, the *Daily Mail*'s social diarist Nigel Dempster printed her picture under the headline 'Has Charles found his Future Bride?' and her short private life was over. From then on there was always a bank of cameras lying in wait for her. Only the following day, at the kindergarten where she worked, Diana was tricked by the photographers into posing against the light in the flimsy see-through skirt that so famously revealed her legs. The reporters came up with their predictable headline – 'Lady Diana's Slip!' – and she bit her lip. She had learnt her first sharp lesson in the public eye: the need for suitable clothes. 'I was so nervous about the whole thing, I never thought I'd be standing with the light right behind me,' she said. 'I don't want to be remembered for not having a petticoat.'

However, it did her no harm with the public, who were prompted for the first time to feel protective of her. 'No other girl in the whole golden company of Charles' steady girlfriends... has had such instant and popular appeal' noted Barbara Griggs in the *Daily Mail*. She was the only journalist who noticed and remarked, in passing, on the pattern of Diana's mauve-and-white printed skirt. In a choice that already marked out her wish to communicate a message without committing herself to words, Diana had chosen to wear a skirt printed with hearts. It was her first deliberate signal, her first communication through fashion.

During the following months Diana clumped along the pavements of Knightsbridge and Pimlico, head bowed and shoulders rounded, trying to evade the press. Like most well-born English girls, she had been brought up in the country, and was more used to muddy Wellington boots than high heels. She was tall – five feet ten inches – and the characteristic tilt of the head was not the flirtatious mannerism it appeared to be, but an attempt not to tower over the men she met. When she was accosted by reporters, she managed to say little or nothing, hanging her head with a sweet, rather coy, one-sided smile.

When it came to the all-important suit for the engagement press photograph, Diana thought of Bellville Sassoon. Belinda Bellville and David Sassoon had made evening dresses for

previous page Head tilted because of her height, gazing out from under a long fringe, Diana showed little sign in the week before her wedding of the scene-stealer she would become. She chose blouses with frilly or scalloped collars, and flimsy gathered skirts with cardigans or waistcoats.

below Soon after the engagement was announced, Diana made an effort to tidy up for the cameras. This red jacket with a black jumper and skirt anticipated the crisper looks of the late eighties.

her mother, and at Mrs Shand Kydd's suggestion Diana dropped into the shop for the first time to have a look. She knew only that she wanted to wear blue, to complement her conspicuously large sapphire-and-diamond engagement ring. Unfortunately for Diana, and for Bellville Sassoon, neither of the designers were in the shop when she went in. She was confronted by the somewhat imposing senior vendeuse, who did not recognize the shy young customer and greeted her with the lofty disdain accorded to women who don't look as though they can afford the goods on offer. Receiving no help, Diana soon walked out again. David Sassoon tells the story ruefully. 'As she left, a young assistant in the shop said "Isn't that the girl who's going to marry Prince Charles?" And so Lady Diana walked away from us, went down the road and bought a suit off the peg.'

The blue suit by Cojana had a scalloped edge and an unbecoming, tight belt. Its print blouse was tied in a large pussy-cat bow to one side, and the skirt covered the knee over thick, patterned tights and flat shoes. Wearing a no-nonsense wristwatch and holding a handbag, Diana looked plump and uncomfortable.

right A couple of months before her wedding, Diana makes an early style statement in polka dots, with a plain red skirt and a trademark piefrill white blouse. The occasion was the first walkabout near Highgrove, the Prince's country house. Red and white spots would remain a favourite for a dozen more years.

Her contact with *Vogue* came about through Felicity Clark, the Beauty Director, whose friendship with Diana's elder sisters, Jane and Sarah, had led to them both working at the magazine for brief periods. Felicity Clark knew Diana as the younger sister of her former assistant, Jane, and was responsible for Diana's earliest appearance in the magazine. She featured alongside the Countess of Halifax and the Honorable Louisa Napier in *Vogue*'s annual spring round-up of pretty debutantes. Taken by Snowdon – the former husband of Princess Margaret – that picture was the first of 142 photographs of Diana that British *Vogue* was to publish over the years. The Snowdon portraits continued, with Felicity Clark as Editor, to mark the engagement, Diana's twenty-first birthday and the births of William in 1982 and Harry in 1984.

opposite Vogue provided this rose pink blouse for Diana's first official portrait by Snowdon. Diana loved it, and asked to meet the designers, David and Elizabeth Emanuel, who would go on to make the wedding dress.

That first photograph was taken before the rumours began about Diana and Prince Charles. By sheer good luck, *Vogue* published the feature in February, the very month in which the engagement was announced. Not long afterwards, Mrs Shand Kydd rang Felicity to ask if the magazine could help Diana find the clothes she needed. Her mother explained that every time her daughter went in a shop, she was embarrassed if she didn't buy anything. The Beauty Director spoke to the Editor-in-Chief, Beatrix Miller, who responded by asking one of her fashion editors, the trustworthy Anna Harvey, to trawl London for the best of everything for Diana to choose from. The idea was never that *Vogue* should advise or guide Diana. They only intended to provide a clothes vocabulary from which Diana could 'shop' according to her needs, and make her own fashion statements. 'In the early days, we didn't know what was expected.' said Anna Harvey. 'There were so many functions and we also had to get a trousseau together. My first thought was tea at Balmoral, because she told me that the royal family changed for afternoon tea.'

below 'Has Charles found his future bride?' wrote *Daily Mail* diarist Nigel Dempster. The kindergarten assistant, photographed with her charges the following day, made her first fashion blunder, with the see-through Laura Ashley skirt that allowed photographers to show her legs. She chose sweet-pea colours, peep-toe shoes and a pattern of hearts.

left and below Diana's first Ascot, in 1981. She dressed up in Bellville Sassoon's scarlet jacket and striped pussy-cat bow, and went to town on accessories. The designers wanted her to simplify the look, but could not find a way to tell her.

Diana came into *Vogue* for the first time with her mother, Mrs Frances Shand Kydd. They arrived, as she always would, from the discreet basement garage, coming up to the fifth floor in the back lift. From there it was only a few steps into Beatrix Miller's large, well lit office overlooking St George Street. The room was now an Aladdin's cave of clothes racks, with shoes, hats and bags stacked against every wall. For Diana, who had spent so little of her life shopping, it was a revelation. 'I don't think she had any idea how many lovely things there were out there' says Anna Harvey. 'Her enthusiasm was contagious.'

'The special thing that Anna did was to coordinate everything,' says Mrs Shand Kydd. It saved hours of shopping to try and find the bags and shoes that would look right with the clothes.

On other visits to Vogue House during this engagement period, she would turn up with her protection officer in tow, and once she ran in through the big glass front doors on Hanover Square, before she could be spotted in her pale-yellow cotton dungarees.

Her official debut came in March, when she accompanied Prince Charles to a recital in the City of London to raise money for the Royal Opera House. 1981 was the year of the full-skirted frilly taffeta evening dress, as celebrated at around the same time by Tina Brown's *Tatler* in a legendary fashion feature called 'Not Safe in Taxis'. The fashion designers Elizabeth and David Emanuel, fresh out of college and majoring in rustling frills, were just beginning to make their mark out of their new first-floor premises in Brook Street.

Pleased with a pink blouse and matching skirt the Emanuels had supplied through Anna Harvey for an early Snowdon sitting, Diana rang them two days after the portrait, to make an appointment. She wanted a strapless taffeta dress in black. Engaged to a man twelve years her senior, the first impulse of the nineteen year old was to try to look older and more sophisticated. 'Black to me was the smartest colour you could possibly have at the age of nineteen,' she said later. 'It was a real grown-up dress.'

'She put on our sample – which had been worn once or twice already – and that was it!' says Elizabeth Emanuel today. 'She was so young she was a little naive in her enthusiasm. None of us saw it as a revealing dress.'

Being a sample, the dress, pretty enough in itself, did not fit like a glove. On this occasion, Anna Harvey was not present to suggest alterations, and Diana had already started to lose weight. The press was so far ignorant of her eating disorder, assuming her slimmer figure was due to routine bridal anxiety. The photographers could not believe their luck as Diana bent to emerge from the Rolls.

Prince Charles had been alarmed into defensive bravado. 'Wait till you get a load of what's coming next,' he told the press as he preceded her out of the car. The next day the palace reverberated with the Queen's displeasure. Not only was the dress too revealing but, in the royal mind, black spells mourning. The press were kinder, 'If this is how she means to go on, then Lady Diana Spencer shows evidence of becoming the most fashion-conscious member of the royal family,' was a typical reaction. The infamous black taffeta was the first indication that Diana would depart from routine royal clothing and experiment, making striking and original fashion choices.

above For a Cowdray Park polo match, Diana wore the pale yellow dungarees that were her favourite outfit of summer 1981. She even wore them to *Vogue*, when she called in to choose clothes.

opposite The infamous low-cut taffeta dress that Diana wore for her first official engagement with Prince Charles. She wanted to wear black because she thought it would make her look sophisticated. She chose a sample from stock at the Emanuels. The press photographers made much of it, the Palace was annoyed and it was a long time before Diana dared to wear a low-cut neckline again.

32

above Relaxed clothes to conceal
pre-wedding nerves: at
Balmoral, Diana's body
language betrays the stress. She
wears one of her collection of
bright patterned sweaters with
trousers by Margaret Howell.

To any fashion editor of the early eighties, the focus was on style parodies
of the fifties and sixties. Fortunately for Diana, there was also a more decorative
and less aggressive look on view in the magazines, and one closer to
establishment hearts with its dandy associations. Diana wore sailor collars,
dressing like the doomed daughters of the Czar of Russia, and picked up on
lace ruffles and velvets for evening, with buckled and bowed shoes and hats
with flying feathers for daytime. Then she went one further with
knickerbockers. These, designed for shooting, had followed riding boots, riding
macs and divided skirts to town, where they were to be seen on what were
now called 'Mayfair Mercenaries' – glamorous girls on the hunt for eligible

men with titles and country estates. Since the eighteenth century, country clothes had been making their way into Mayfair and the City, where the new generation had just coined the word 'fogey' to describe the young man in his boldly striped shirt and traditional tailoring, topped with his father's prickly tweed coat and his grandfather's hat. There was even a Fulham shop called Hackett, where pretenders could buy these clothes second hand, and where you could find a long rail of Barbours, the shooting waterproofs that were virtually Sloane uniform.

Diana's knickerbockers were corduroy, and she wore them with her trademark ruffled shirt. The *Daily Mail* ran a fashion feature called 'Follow the Leader', in which they tracked down cheap high-street copies of the look and

left The piecrust frill becomes a Diana trademark in 1981, as copies of her clothes go into high street shops.

Princess Diana

right A favourite off-the-peg outfit from Roland Klein: white pleated skirt and cotton sweater, with a navy scarf knitted in and stitched with rhinestones. Diana wore this on a number of occasions from 1981 to 1987.

photographed them on a Diana lookalike. There would be many more Diana rip-offs as the eighties progressed.

Meanwhile Diana was undergoing a crash course in designer London. Whenever she could, she would drop in to Roland Klein's shop, at that time beneath the Emanuels, and pick clothes off the shelf, her protection officer remaining outside in the car. One of her favourite outfits from Klein's shop was a pleated white linen skirt and a navy cotton sweater, with a trompe l'oeil white scarf knitted in and decorated with rhinestones. She often returned to favourite outfits and was still wearing this when she took Harry to a royal family party at Windsor in 1987. 'I wanted to tell Lady Diana to improve her posture, but I didn't have the guts,' says Roland Klein today.

For her going away outfit, she went back to Bellville Sassoon, this time accompanied firmly by her mother. But although her mother made some of the introductions, she did not exert undue influence over her daughter.

'I did what a mother does on these occasions,' says Mrs Frances Shand Kydd. 'I took her to fashion houses and a number of shops in London where I felt comfortable, and which provided clothes that she liked wearing. All children pick up something from their mothers, but I was simply there to introduce her to certain designers and she took it from there.

'We had a lot of fun – and I acquired some clothes for myself along the way, including what I wore to the wedding.'

Diana chose an unusual colour for the outfit. Somewhere between terracotta and apricot, the name of the shade she asked for was 'cantaloupe'. On the day, the outfit was reported to be a suit with a big organdie collar, and an ostrich feathered hat. The collar actually belonged to the knee-length dress beneath, with a cummerbund sash, and the jacket was a short-sleeved bolero. In case the weather was bad, Diana had ordered two jackets for the dress. Six months later she was to take the long-sleeved version on the tour to Australia.

left and opposite Diana's going-away outfit by Bellville Sassoon was ordered with two jackets – one with short sleeves, one with long. She wore the short-sleeved version on her wedding day, and the other for her first major official overseas trip to Australia in 1982. She matched it with a hat by John Boyd, and celebrated her new rank with a Prince of Wales ostrich plume.

As always, when particularly pleased with a garment, or when the designer had gone out of his way to make something special or complicated, she sent a hand-written, thank-you letter immediately. Her bills were promptly paid by the Prince of Wales' office, and signed 'Charles'. She was given no special deals, and if a designer failed to bill her, a lady-in-waiting would telephone with a reminder.

In a vote of confidence, in her own choice no less than their ability, Diana went back to the Emanuels for her wedding dress. 'We had to keep it secret,' remembers Elizabeth Emanuel. 'The urge to tell everyone was overpowering! The only person we did tell early on was my father, who was in hospital waiting to have a quadrupal bypass operation. He'd backed us financially, and this was a kind of justification for his confidence in us. It was a very moving moment. His face lit up!'

The dress was made in a locked room by a single seamstress, Nina Missetzis, and passed into history on 29 July 1981. It was made of 45 feet of ivory silk taffeta, and trimmed with antique Carrick-Ma-Cross lace, presented by Queen Mary to the Royal School of Needlework. The 25-foot veil and train, securely held by the ravishing Spencer diamond tiara, was hand sewn with ten thousand mother-of-pearl sequins. With full sleeves, frills and bows it was gathered into a voluminous, rustling crinoline that proved almost too large for the confines of the carriage that took her to St Paul's. At every fitting, Diana was found to have lost weight again, her waist decreasing from 29 inches to 23½ inches between the first and last fittings. Finally, after the bodice had been taken in several times, it was too late to make more adjustments.

The mystique of the dress was magnified by the details, relayed in every newspaper to an avid readership. As advised by Maureen Baker, who had made Princess Anne's wedding dress, the Emanuels incorporated the superstitious ancient traditions of the dressmaker's trade, tucking a blue bow inside the bodice. Diana borrowed diamond earrings from her mother and, for luck, a tiny gold horseshoe, encrusted with diamonds, was sewn into the waist. The Emanuels were asked by the Palace to make two of the dress. The copy, made with certain economies, was to be worn by Diana's effigy in Madame Tussaud's, London's famous wax museum.

Diana had moved somewhat reluctantly into Clarence House, the London home of the Queen Mother, after the engagement was announced. It was there that, early on the day of the wedding, the Emanuels joined the seamstress, the make-up artist and the hairdresser to get her ready.

previous pages, above and right
Diana and the Emanuels set
out to design an elaborate
extravaganza of a wedding
dress appropriate for a fairytale
marriage to a prince. Looking
back at her wedding dress in
1997, a sadder but wiser
woman, Diana was to say
that she hoped to find that the
moths had reduced the volume.

'Diana was joking around and singing "Just one cornetto!"' remembers Elizabeth Emanuel. 'We kept looking from the screen out of the window on to the crowds in the Mall, to see the reality. She was on top form. She was really excited.'

Any bride in a white wedding dress, whether deliberately or not, is sending out pagan messages of virginity, dedication, sacrifice and promise. This exuberant, Victorian-style dress was intended by Diana to signal a fairy-tale conclusion to what, we later came to realize, was a barely satisfactory royal romance. The dress ushered in the sentiment of all fairy tales that end with marriage to a prince '...and they lived happily ever after'.

Looking back on that day, a sadder woman, Diana was to say 'I remember being so in love with my husband that I couldn't take my eyes off him. I just absolutely thought I was the luckiest girl in the world.'

In a postscript that presaged Diana's future power over the fashion industry, bridal manufacturers applied themselves to duplicating the dress in record time. Within five hours of the wedding there were already two copies of the dress in Oxford Street stores.

Public Education

'The first time Lady Diana visited my shop, she came on a bicycle, carrying a basket,' says Manolo Blahnik, shoemaker of distinction. 'After the wedding, she came by car, with her driver, and we would empty the shop and close up while she was with us.'

When Diana returned to London after the prolonged honeymoon on the Royal Yacht *Britannia* and at Balmoral, she was a changed woman. That is to say, like so many people who suddenly achieve a high profile, she found all the changes in other people. 'People called me "Ma'am" now,' she said '... but I treated everyone else exactly the same.'

'Overnight, she had become HRH,' says David Sassoon. 'We naturally accorded her the full royal treatment.' Knee joints cracked as middle-aged fitters curtsied their way into the fitting rooms and backed out, curtsying again.

Designers less used to royal customers found the etiquette difficult, particularly in view of Diana's continuing informality. She still sat on the floor to look at sketches and treated everyone with equal consideration. '*Vogue* reminded me to curtsy and say "Ma'am",' says the tailor Margaret Howell, who made corduroy trousers and tweed suits for the Princess in the early eighties. 'Diana had asked me to make up a piece of tweed she had been given into a pair of breeches. I think she was going to revisit the people who had given it to her. When I got to the Palace and Diana came bounding up the stairs, and then went behind the sofa to try them on, I just felt I didn't need to do those things.'

previous page On honeymoon at Balmoral the Princess wore a brown tweed suit by Bill Pashley and Chelsea Cobbler shoes with bare legs tanned brown on the deck of the royal yacht *Britannia*. Diana looked great, but a touch too smart for the Highlands – more suitably dressed for a Sunday stroll in Hyde Park. The clothes were pre-selected for her by *Vogue* magazine.

The photographers now watched Diana's regular haunts. She only had to appear at an event for a crowd to collect, the street to come to a standstill and her protection officers to become concerned for her safety. After a few experiments, it was agreed that she could no longer attend fashion shows. Victor Edelstein then had the idea of inviting her and her lady-in-waiting, Anne Beckwith Smith, to attend the rehearsal instead and so the dress rehearsal became much smarter than the show itself.

The designers more often went to Kensington Palace – 'POW at KP' as they wrote in their diaries – with drawings and fabric samples, or a half-finished garment ready to be pinned. Diana had no reservations about undressing to try on the clothes. Some of the more reverential designers were embarrassed by this. 'I made for the door,' says one, 'she called out "Stay!" and so I crossed over to the window and stared out fixedly.'

London's top fashion designers, from milliners to cobblers, are great characters: amusing, gossipy, urbane, camp and good dinner-party material. Deprived of her circle of jolly girlfriends, and finding herself in a marriage where most of the affection was on her side, it is not surprising that Diana took solace in their company. There was probably no other professional group

left On her first visit to Wales as its Princess, Diana revived the John Boyd ostrich feather hat she had worn with her going-away outfit as a tribute to the Welsh people: the Prince of Wales' badge consists of three ostrich plumes. With her thick fringe, ostrich feathers and decorative neckline, she needed to streamline her image.

with whom Diana found such companionship until her later involvement with the workers of the charities she endorsed. She could be less guarded in fashion circles than almost anywhere, secure in the knowledge that the designers understood that indiscretion would spell the end of the patronage. If she didn't trust them, she didn't stay with them.

Diana was the ideal British fashion client and it was clear that she was a royal whose glamour potential could be of movie-star proportions. To dress her brought great rewards, both in terms of prestige and profit. For Diana it was in the line of duty to go shopping, but the pleasure she took in adding variety to the royal fashion formulas was equalled by her enjoyment of the designers' company. For them, too, there was something more than opportunism at work. 'One wanted to help her, she engaged your loyalty and affection,' says David Sassoon. 'She was so trusting and charming.'

By her demeanour and her few telling asides, the designers knew better than anyone else at this early stage that something was wrong. There are many stories of tears in the fitting room. As a result, they felt protective of her and she responded to this with appreciation.

The talented designer, Victor Edelstein, now an artist and portrait-painter, was to make some of Diana's most famous dresses. He found himself deeply

above The public engagements were building up, and Diana did not have enough clothes. When she asked David Sassoon to design her a coat, he offered her five sketches and was surprised when she ordered them all. This, in blue wool gathered from the yoke and with puff sleeves, was worn on an official visit to Brixton, south London in 1981.

moved by her plight. 'Some of the clothes she liked in the early eighties were rather "girly" and not very me,' he says. 'But I didn't say anything about it. I really liked her, and she was so pushed around at the Palace that I used to feel that I wasn't going to push her around too.' On a Christmas visit to Kensington Palace at this time, he found her, pale and thin, forlornly trying to cope with a Christmas tree that had dropped its needles on the carpet. 'That particular day she seemed so young and fragile. I thought, "the poor thing, she's got nobody to help her," and I hoped she would be all right.'

The gentle Scotsman John Boyd, Princess Anne's milliner and a royal favourite, made Diana small decorative hats of the kind her mother had bought from him. The feathered hat he had made for her going away outfit entered milliners' language in 1981 as the 'Lady Di' shape. He had met Diana with her mother some time before her engagement, and always saw her in the same way. 'To me, she was a poor wee lassie dressing up in her mother's clothes,' he says fondly. 'I knew the palace rigmarole, I knew she would have to buckle down soon enough, so we let her play with the hats. I thought, "enjoy yourself while you can."'

left Pale and thin, Diana looked almost childlike in this tweed and velvet coat and beret on a visit to Liverpool in 1981. Bulimic and depressed, her grey mood showed through. Faced with the task of dressing her for confidence in the new royal role, the designers felt protective and anxious about the forlorn twenty-year-old.

above Splashing through puddles
on the Welsh tour of 1981,
in a Caroline Charles coat
tied like a dressing gown,
Diana was suffering from
morning sickness. However,
she braved the wet Welsh
weather to greet the crowds
who had come to see her.

Diana was equally fond of him. Once, when her protection officer had accompanied her into Boyd's workshop, he had begun to give his opinions uninvited: 'That one's all wrong! This one's better.' Concerned that the milliner's feelings would be hurt, she waited until the officer had returned downstairs, and said quietly, 'You won't see *him* again.'

Boyd was allowed to tease the Princess as nobody else would have done. She startled him one day by turning up at his shop in knickerbockers, asking if she could go upstairs to have a look in the workroom. 'I told her, "You're wearing rompers, and wee laddies are not allowed up there."'

Jasper Conran, who had been a target for the press himself, became a friend of the Princess, meeting her for lunch occasionally, saw her as, 'horribly harrassed by the palace machine. She was ticked off and told off by the men in grey suits. Then there was the press. She sometimes asked me, "How do I cope? How does anyone cope?"' He concluded that she had no one to talk to who had encountered the problems she was facing, and so was always looking for people she could ask about managing the media.

She was given no royal coaching whatsoever, but everyone expected her to know just what to do and how to perform. At first, she was very short of suitable clothes. Switching on the Regent Street Christmas lights in 1981, early in her first pregnancy, she was wearing navy culottes that she could not button up. She had nothing else to wear. She learned to buy clothes in quantity, knowing that she would often have to change four times in a day. When she told David Sasson that she wanted a coat, the designer sketched five, thinking she would choose one. Instead, she said, 'I'll have them all.'

below Reverting to teenage dressing at polo matches, Diana tried spotted bobby socks with high heels to match her Mondi skirt. The designers groaned, but Diana studied her cuttings and was careful not to make this sort of mistake again.

She had to learn fast. Ever since the fuss about the low-cut black taffeta dress she had worn for her first public engagement, she was wary of low strapless necklines. From the palace came the odd criticism, but no constructive help. She had to find out for herself the tricks of royal fashion etiquette, and decide which applied to her and which did not.

She discovered that skirts could be weighted like curtains, so that they did not blow up as she emerged from a helicopter or stood on a dais in the open air. She found that the photographers uttered groans of disappointment when her hat brims were allowed to obscure her face. She learned just how tight a skirt could be and still allow her to get out of a car elegantly. So much had been taken for granted by the royal family since the twenties. Other rules were learnt, then gradually discarded. 'Royals wear bright colours so you can pick them out in a crowd,' says Bruce Oldfield. 'As I pointed out to the Princess, most of them are 5 feet 4 inches tall. When you're blonde and 6 feet 3 inches in high heels you could wear a sack and you would stand out!'

above left With her young face framed in diamonds, a better haircut and wearing a pale and delicate evening dress like this one in frilled cream organza with pintucks and lace by Gina Fratini, Diana looked prettier than ever before on this tour of New Zealand in 1983, where she reacted to the public adulation with a rapid increase in confidence.

above right The ruffled silk maternity dress in pale blue with white spots, worn here at a polo match just before William's birth, was one that Diana chose from a Catherine Walker brochure. It was one of her first dresses by the designer who would make so much of her wardrobe in the years to come.

Sometimes Diana regressed to dressing like a teenager, most conspicuously on the semi-public sidelines of Charles' polo matches where she was seen in creased cotton dungarees, or bobby socks with high heels. In those early days, designers such as Jasper Conran would groan when they saw their suit or coat put together with the wrong hat or frilly blouse. 'She needed paring down and simplifying, but there was no chance to tell her.' Bruce Oldfield, who began making suits for her during this period, thinks that she was buying from too many designers and mixing their clothes indiscriminately. 'She needed a stylist!' he says. 'She went off into fashion like a loose cannon – like a kid in a sweetshop. One day a big gown, the next a horrible fussy hat.' On the other hand, dressing for Diana was more complicated than it was for other people. 'The fashion police were saying, "Doesn't she know better?" I wanted to say, "Hold on! This is the future Queen of England. Don't judge her by your standards."'

No one was more aware of her fashion mistakes than Diana herself, as she studied her photographs in newspapers and magazines. If a criticism was made, she adjusted accordingly. She took to wearing flattering big, bright sweaters with narrow leg jeans for watching polo, and had the satisfaction of reading about her dazzling glamour and charisma in the newspapers on the following day. In a radical reaction to the criticism she had received for the low-cut black taffeta, she compensated on her next public evening appearance with a high Puritan collar on a long-sleeved, knee-covering velvet dress by Gina Fratini. It was November 1981, and it had just been announced that she was pregnant. She was so thin inside the voluminous dress that the *Daily Mail* asked Professor Sir Jack Dewhurst, of the University of London and Queen Charlotte's Hospital if it would make for a difficult pregnancy. 'The Princess' continued weight loss is not a pointer to any pregnancy problems,' Dewhurst assured the British public. 'I believe the excitement and changes in settling down to her new life are responsible.'

above A few months after William's birth, Diana became thinner than she had ever been. To the première of *ET* she wore a taffeta dress with a strapless velvet bodice. When she took off the accompanying velvet bolero, she exposed painfully bony shoulders and arms, alerting the press to her bulimia.

left Diana's passion for taffeta crinolines continued after her wedding. Here, two months from William's birth at a function at the Barbican in London, she wears scarlet taffeta lined with white lace ruffles. Framed in the neckline was a fabulous diamond drop necklace given to the Queen by an Arab prince, and loaned to Diana for the night. Diana eventually owned a jewellery collection estimated at £17 million.

51

Diana discovered that she was pregnant on the eve of her first tour, in October 1981. The royal family were delighted, and for a short time she was the centre of attention. Suffering from a combination of bulimia and morning sickness, she was in no condition to enjoy it. She looked tired and strained as she accompanied Charles to Wales and noted, 'Wrong clothes, wrong everything, wrong timing, feeling terribly sick.' It rained constantly, and by the second day her long fringe had flopped under her jaunty little hats by John Boyd. Responding to the crowds, who had waited for hours in the pouring rain to see her, she emerged from an umbrella and splashed through puddles to accept flowers, conscientiously murmuring '*diolch*', the Welsh for 'thank you'. Wearing a Caroline Charles oatmeal coat wrapped and tied like a dressing gown, with wet ostrich feathers sticking to her cheek, she did her best to shake every hand. She even made a speech in Welsh, and hoped in vain for a word of congratulation from her husband.

Expecting her first baby, Diana asked David Sassoon to make most of her maternity clothes. 'I was surprised,' he says. 'It wasn't my thing, and she didn't really know what she wanted.' He made her several dresses which she turned into more formal outfits for her engagements by adding little veiled hats – but, as Sassoon comments, 'Maternity dresses never do look right with hats. She was still trying to conform to royal rules. Later, when she was expecting Harry, she decided to break the rules and go hatless. That was much better.' Jan Vanvelden made her favourite maternity tops and skirts. After Harry's birth, Diana asked him to adapt them so that she could go on wearing them.

Later in the pregnancy, three months before William's birth, she looked blooming in a frilled claret taffeta dress. Its square neck framed a diamond-drop necklace she had borrowed for the occasion

below and opposite During and between her pregnancies, Diana wore many of Jan Vanvelden's designs. The Dutchman liked to frame her face in big puritan collars, as though she was a Van Dyke portrait. For her pregnancies, he made gathered skirts on basques of sheer elastic. Diana liked these so much she asked him to adapt them after Harry's birth so that she could go on wearing them.

opposite and right For a few years, Diana's diplomatic signals were a little heavy-handed. For the Braemar games she wore plenty of tartan, and John Boyd made her a Scots soldier's Glengarry. It was a little too much like costume design.

from the Queen. By contrast she had never been so thin as in the interval between pregnancies.

The age gap between Diana and Charles produced misplaced expectations on both sides. She expected love, guidance and protection. He expected loyalty, support and commitment to royal interests. The rumours began, but Charles only had to kiss his wife's hand on the polo field and any rumours were dispelled. 'Gossip and stress took their toll on young Diana' was a typical press reaction. 'Love saw them through early storms.'

At first, no setbacks could alter her resolve to perform correctly.

She had begun to incorporate into her clothes certain elements that would appeal to people in a particular way, according to the place and the event. At first, her signals were a little heavy-handed. For the first few years, she rarely set foot in Scotland without dressing from head to foot in tartan. There was, for instance, the plaid outfit by Caroline Charles that she wore with a John Boyd hat modelled on a soldier's Glengarry, with flying ribbons at the back. At Boyd's suggestion, she pinned a brooch in place of the regimental badge. In Wales, she wore a red and green suit to match the Welsh flag. Boyd, with little time to prepare, whipped a green band around a red hat she had worn with a Bellville Sassoon dress on an earlier date. He recalls, 'She stuck it on the back of her head this time, to make it look different.' This is an

left and opposite Diana had a doll-like prettiness in this dress by Bellville Sassoon, with pale blue satin bows and sash. She wore it to the opening of the Gonzaga exhibition at the Victoria and Albert Museum, where – pregnant with William – she momentarily fell asleep on a chair. She was immediately forgiven.

early example of Diana reworking her clothes, exercising ingenuity to disguise the fact she had worn them before.

In her efforts to help Diana, *Vogue*'s Anna Harvey would sometimes order a dress for her, and pass on the measurements. It soon became apparent that dressmaking is a thing that cannot be done via a middleman. Over the four years after her wedding, Diana's weight was as volatile as her emotions, fluctuating between the extremes brought about by two pregnancies alternating with bouts of bulimia and morning sickness. Her arms were rather long and during these early years, because of bad posture, she had a curved back which designers also had to take into account in fittings. When Diana was expecting William, Victor Edelstein was given a set of measurements and asked to make an evening dress for her in pink taffeta. 'The measurements looked strange to me, and the dress was a disaster,' he recalls. 'I was invited to go to the palace

and see if it could be fixed. She put on the dress, and it was a monster. We both had to laugh.'

Through all her tribulations, she had become much prettier. She had a more flattering hairstyle than the pudding-basin cut of 1980, and was as slim as a model. In those early years she never looked better than on big, formal evening occasions when she would be dressed in a white or pale-coloured confection of frills and tucks, often by Gina Fratini, and glittering with jewels. One of her most charming early evening dresses was the Bellville Sassoon dress she wore to the Gonzaga exhibition at the Victoria and Albert Museum in 1981: frosted chiffon hand-painted with glitter, the bodice a shoulder-to-shoulder frill with pale-blue bows to match the sash.

With her perfect skin and beautiful eyes, she had an almost childlike bloom in the fabulous tiara that the Queen had given her for a wedding present. Made for Queen Mary, this was a diamond halo of lovers' knots with large pearl drops. Somtimes she might wear the emeralds, also given to her by the Queen, with Charles' gift of an art deco emerald-and-diamond bracelet to match, or a selection from the suite of sapphires and diamonds given as a wedding present by the Crown Prince of Saudi Arabia. When the occasion demanded, she wore the Queen's royal family order, a miniature portrait of the sovereign in a diamond border on a chartreuse-yellow watered silk riband.

Later Diana would be more chic, more fashionable and more elegant, but she would never again be so enchantingly fresh. She already knew how to cast her spell around a room, so that people could not take their eyes off her. She liked to reach out to people, ready to put a hand on their arm, or respond to a handshake. Anna Harvey delivered dozens of pairs of suede gloves to Kensington Palace, because the royals were seldom seen without gloves. 'Heaven knows where they all went, because she never wore any of them. She wanted flesh-to-flesh contact.' It was a short step from there to the request she made when ordering a suit for visiting a charity for the blind. She wanted it in velvet, so that she would feel soft and friendly to their touch.

She had been brought up to be polite and well mannered, but she also radiated pleasure in human contact. 'She knew people were desperate to meet her,' remembers Jasper Conran of her visits. 'When she came here, she wanted to meet everyone in the building. She knew you simply couldn't leave anyone out.'

below At a fashion show in 1982, Diana meant the press to write about her one-shoulder ruffled dress. They wrote instead about her skeletal appearance. Her bulimia was particularly bad in 1982, after the birth of William, and she had never been thinner than she was between her pregnancies.

'She knew she had that magnetic appeal, even in the early eighties,' says Bruce Oldfield. 'When people drew near to her, she turned to them with these lovely little asides – not with that stony royal response. She knew she could increase that power through her frocks, and she was becoming fixated on the way she was looking.'

In 1983, Diana took on what she called, 'the real hard end of being the Princess of Wales' as she embarked on a six-week tour of Australia and New Zealand with Charles. The Australian Prime Minister, Malcolm Fraser, encouraged her to bring baby William along. This delighted her, although in the event she did not see much of him. 'At least we were under the same sky,' she said. By the time they arrived in Australia, Fraser had been replaced as Prime Minister.

She was jet-lagged, homesick and oppressed by the huge numbers of press. There were times when all she wanted to do was fly home.

above left Bruce Oldfield's turquoise and silver dress ruffled down each side was a dress that only the slimmest of women could have worn. Diana wore it on the Australia tour in 1983 and dazzled the company.

'I was thrown into the deep end,' she said. 'Nobody helped me at all ... but when we came back, I was a different person.' In spite of everything, the tour was a spectacular success. Her clothes had played their part in the warmth of the public reaction. She wore eight outfits by Vanvelden the Dutchman, many with puritan collars. At a charity ball in Sydney, she took to the floor in Bruce Oldfield's pale-blue and silver chiffon dress to dance a fast foxtrot with Charles; in New Zealand, in a pale-blue veiled hat, she bent to rub noses with a Maori woman. For the first time, he had to accustom himself to groans of disappointment from the crowd when he, and not Diana, advanced to meet them. She had eclipsed him and it added to the pressure on the marriage. In one of his speeches, he turned it into a joke – 'If only I had two wives, to cover both sides of the street' – but in private he could not hide his jealousy.

Pregnancy brought the first contact with the designer who would do so much for her over the following sixteen years. In November 1981, two months pregnant with William, she ordered some maternity dresses from Catherine Walker, and went back for more when she was expecting Harry. David Sassoon made her a couple of very successful maternity 'function' dresses. One, a tunic-style evening dress in cream sparkling chiffon, with a boat neck and a narrow skirt to the floor, was one of the most sophisticated dresses she had yet worn. The other, a blue velvet dress, was made for her to wear with the Saudi sapphires. The wide neck and cuffs were trimmed with Queen Victoria's antique lace, found at Balmoral. 'The Duchess of Kent had brought it in for trimming the hem of one of her dresses, and this piece was left over. We said to the Princess – when the dress wears out, save the collar!'

right Jan Vanvelden designed several maternity outfits for Diana, among them this Liberty print suit in fine wool with a puritan collar and blue bow. She wore this in May 1984, when she was expecting Harry.

Jasper Conran made her a favourite white mohair jacket which she wore several times with his dresses at polo. 'No matter what you were making for her,' he says, 'the question was always "Will my husband think I'm sexy in this?" Between pregnancies, she had become absolutely obsessed with a slim line. But even when I was making maternity dresses for her, the question was the same. I found it very sad.'

Over these early years, the unhappiness showed through, although it was perhaps not as unrelieved as has since been suggested. There are moments caught on camera, usually on the polo field, which are undeniably of a couple happy and affectionate in each other's company. As Diana was to say 'We were very, very close to each other the six weeks before Harry was born, the closest we've ever, ever been and ever will be. Then suddenly as Harry was born it just went bang, our marriage, the whole thing went down the drain.'

above Diana now looked relaxed on the sidelines of Prince Charles' polo matches. Here she wears a favourite white mohair jacket by Jasper Conran.

right Diana wore this spotted peach silk tunic and skirt by Jan Vanvelden during and after her pregnancy, here at Ascot in 1985. Vanvelden originally made the skirt on a basque yoke or ruched elastic, and remade it afterwards as Diana lost weight. She told the designer his skirts were the most comfortable she had ever worn.

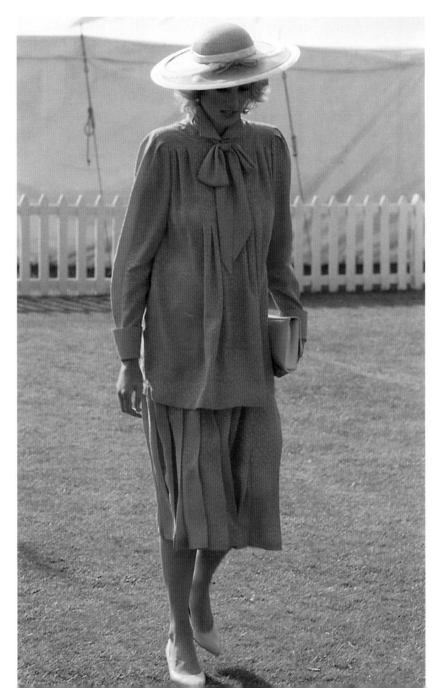

above Pictured here at a polo
match at Cirencester Park in
1985, with her Laura Ashley
blouse and bouffant hair, Diana
appears confident and in love,
in spite of the rumours about
her unhappy state.

Partial Eclipse

For Diana, the three years after Harry's birth were difficult years of isolation and competition. Charles admitted that he was now in regular contact with Camilla Parker-Bowles again – 'Do you seriously expect me to be the first Prince of Wales in British history not to have a mistress?' – and Diana's boisterous new sister-in-law, Prince Andrew's bride Sarah Ferguson, had captivated the public and charmed the royal family.

For the first time, Diana was receiving a bad press. As the *Sunday Times* expressed it in the summer of 1987: 'When Prince Andrew married Sarah Ferguson the public agreed that Fergie was a jolly nice girl and she could never hope to compete with the glamorous Princess of Wales. Twelve months have changed the picture. To palace insiders, who have seen Fergie blossom and Diana decline, the only question is how long the Princess can hold her own against the extrovert new Duchess?' The newspapers compared the troubled Diana with the confident, cheery Fergie and decided that Diana was self-absorbed, and a mere fashion plate. 'Fergie will never have Diana's model-girl figure or fashion-plate looks, but she is learning to dress with charm.'

The high-spirited Duchess encouraged Diana to liven up the stuffy royal proceedings. Charles, who had formerly held up the Queen Mother as an example to Diana, now started asking her 'Why can't you be more like Fergie?' In the knowledge that Fergie was a royal and public favourite, Diana abandoned caution. The sisters-in-law embarked on a series of larks that began with dressing up as policewomen and bursting in on Prince Andrew's stag party. Unfortunately for the Princess of Wales, they were judged by a double standard. Though outwardly rowdy and unguarded, Fergie was judged by the royal family to be 'sound'. Though generally well behaved and self-contained in public, Diana was thought, on account of her bulimia and tears, to be 'uncontrolled'. Meanwhile, the royal duties were building up for Diana, who was expected to buckle down to some 130 public engagements a year – only about 20 fewer than the Queen. Comparing herself with the Duchess, Diana may have found herself envying the freedom of her pre-marital years and the three love affairs that Fergie enjoyed before her engagement. The result was, in Diana's own words, 'I got terribly jealous and she got terribly jealous of me'. In the nicest and most civilized way possible, fashion became the territory over which they fought.

above, right and opposite This single-sleeved and draped cream chiffon dress, by the late fashion designer Hachi, was given as a present to Diana by *Vogue's* Anna Harvey. It was the Princess's first narrow and sophisticated evening dress, and it marked a cooler and more elegant phase in her fashion life. With its crystal and transparent gold glass embroidery it became one of her favourite dresses.

previous page Diana wore this finely pleated pale blue chiffon dress and stole to the Cannes Film Festival in 1987, a movie buff's reference to the one that Grace Kelly had worn in Hitchcock's *To Catch a Thief*. It was made by Catherine Walker.

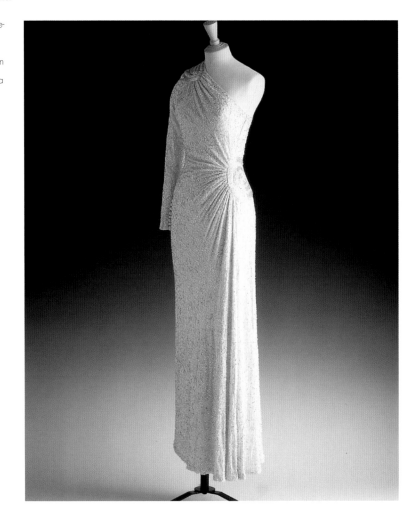

above On a skiing holiday in Klosters in 1987 Fergie proved herself the better skier but Diana's graphic £300 ski suit by Kitex, and knitted white hood put her sister-in-law in the shade. A few minutes after this photograph was taken, the sisters-in-law scuffled in the snow and clowned for the cameras. Charles was not amused.

opposite Everything important about this burgundy crushed velvet dress by Catherine Walker, worn to the première of *Back to the Future* in 1985, happened at the back: a deep V, ruched bustle and satin bow. To complete the effect Diana knotted a string of pearls between her shoulder blades.

When Diana invited the Irish designer and tailor Paul Costelloe to Kensington Palace to show her some sketches, she did not know that Fergie already bought his clothes. When he mentioned the Duchess's name, Diana cut him short. 'Let's say she evinced no pleasure,' he remembers. 'She instantly steered me onto another subject. I didn't make very many clothes for her.'

Diana, who knew that she could always look more beautiful and sophisticated than Fergie, could point to her larger public role as a reason to be exclusive in the matter of designers. If she was vain, she had good reason for it. She could justify the importance of fashion in her life. It would remain her chief channel of communication with the public until 1992. At this phase of her life, Diana came to realize that, intended or unintended, her clothes always provoked public interpretations of her state of mind. If she could not help sending out signals, she had to learn to control them. With more time and money to spend on clothes than almost any other woman alive, she was particularly hurt by the criticisms and exhilarated by the praise. It was her job, and almost her career, to look good.

'Fashion was something that Diana was in the process of making hers,' says Jasper Conran. 'She was territorial about her designers, but not in an unpleasant way. It was as if she was saying "this is a thing I'm building, and it is important." '

When Conran met Fergie at a dinner party, she whispered that she was 'not allowed' to come to him for her clothes. She meant that Conran was Diana's property. Of course, that was an exaggeration, but designers who dress more than one royal customer walk a minefield of potential embarrassments.

above and opposite The strongly striped navy and white suit by Roland Klein with two-tone shoes and a large, simple hat by Philip Somerville stood out clear and strong against the other members of the royal enclosure at Ascot in 1985. Diana was beginning to understand what photographed well and what a tall blonde beauty could get away with.

They have to be meticulous in keeping the orders separate and exclusive, so that a dress can never be duplicated.

Tomasz Starzewski, the society designer who was to specialize in Diana's 'lunch suits', managed to keep her custom until her death, although he also dressed the Duchess of York and several members of international royalty. He even, although there is no reason to suppose that the Princess knew it, made the occasional outfit for Camilla Parker-Bowles.

'We had to be very sure that no other royal ordered the same thing. We had to juggle it,' he says. 'I had to be very clear that it was first come, first served. I told every customer who had what. And when the Princess started ordering from my samples, she and the Duchess were great pals.'

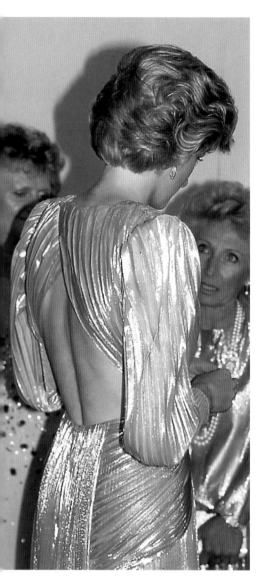

above Diana, who never missed an episode of *Dynasty* or *Dallas*, was labelled 'Dynasty Di' when she experimented with this pleated gold lamé dress by Bruce Oldfield in November 1985: it was not the kind of dress the royals usually wore.

In one respect, Starzewski found it easy to keep Diana's clothes separate. 'The Princess never ran in the same lane as the international crowd,' is how he puts it. 'She was different, and she had a different life. She didn't have a gang of friends, and if you discount her public engagements, she actually didn't have much of a social life. It was rather tragic, but the chance of her finding herself at lunch where another of my customers was wearing the same suit was almost nil.'

In 1987, Fergie, presumably finding too many of London's best designers unavailable to her, made a brief shopping trip to Paris, and to the master himself, Yves Saint Laurent. She returned to London with some of the most elegant clothes she had ever worn: a simple pink jacket over a black dress, and a dark green Edwardian velvet evening dress with green coq feathers in her red hair. The magazines were quick to announce that Fergie had put fashion mistakes behind her. That proved not to be true, but she had come a long way since the clumsily banded frock she wore to Ascot, a botched garment which was so vilified in the fashion press that the unfortunate designer sank without trace and was never heard of again. For the moment, Fergie was perceived as the royal impact-maker in fashion.

The press claimed that Diana was obliged to show support for British fashion, and this had diluted her international impact. Hard as it is to believe now, Diana was dropped from the international best-dressed list in February 1987 because she looked 'too much like a mannequin'. 'Diana tends to be cast in a mould' was a typical press reaction, this from the fashion editor of the *Daily Express*, Jackie Modlinger. 'She is predictably dressed. The only innovations she is creating are in a small way with her hosiery, hats and hairstyle.'

Comments like this were wide of the mark, for Diana's clothes have never ceased to surprise. But it was a period when she simply couldn't win. While Charles could visit his mistress as often as he liked without comment from the newspapers, she was criticized for almost everything she did. If she went with friends to a disco, the newspapers wrote, 'Beyond the Glitter Diana is Drawn to a Seedy World'. If she looked fabulous and the papers failed to mention that Charles was present too, her press coverage got a frosty reception from his office. If she dressed in Dallas-type gold lamé, she was 'Dynasty Di'. If she dressed in a well cut tweed suit with a velvet collar, as she did on the 1985 trip to Australia, the press christened her 'Dowdy Diana' and speculated that she was keeping her best clothes for other events. And when she cropped her hair in 1987 and had it combed into a teddy-boy quiff to go with a peacock satin rock 'n' roll jacket and bootlace tie, the light-hearted experiment was deemed 'disastrous'.

As Roland Klein remembers, 'If the Princess said she wanted the hem above her knees and I said "Are you sure, Ma'am?" she would say to me "Yes, because whatever I do I will be criticized – so let's go for it!"'

It was a time of risk taking and experimentation, a time when her clothes looked so ill assorted that they might have belonged to different people. After her death, her entire remaining wardrobe was left packed into two rooms at Kensington Palace, many of them in the pale blue and white zipped travelling hanger-bags stamped with her initial and crown insignia. In the first room, in the walk-in wardrobe, there is the collection of clothes that she was wearing at the time of her death. In the second, a long narrow room devoted to storage, the clothes occupy the floor space, with hats, bags and accessories on a higher tier that goes up to the ceiling. Grouped together in the late 1980s section are some of the most memorable clothes she ever wore, the notorious experiments and the dignified evening dresses, irrespective of contemporary judgements. There is the policewoman's uniform that Diana wore with Fergie for the stag night prank that so alarmed and annoyed the Queen. There is the puffball miniskirt she wore to the Cannes Film Festival in 1985 that caused

left and above Midnight blue silk tulle was lined with purple silk for this dinner dress by Murray Arbeid. The pleated torso and flaring skirt were embroidered with sparkling stars. Diana wore this to the première of *Phantom of the Opera* and at a private dinner at Claridges in 1986, given by former King Constantine of the Hellenes. Unusually, she wore it with pink evening gloves.

much excited comment. There is the elegant navy-and-white striped Roland Klein suit she wore with a big hat for Ascot in 1987, when she incurred the Queen's displeasure again by giggling her way around the royal enclosure with Fergie, and poking her friend Lulu Blacker in the bottom with the point of her umbrella. There are the skin-tight leather pants by Jasper Conran that she wore when she went to a pop concert without Charles, sitting between Princess Margaret's son David Linley and Major David Waterhouse of the Household Cavalry. 'I went in leather trousers,' she said later 'completely putting out of mind that I was the future Queen and future Queens don't wear leather like that in public. So I thought that was frightfully "with it", frightfully pleased to act my own age.' And there are several dresses with the plunging necklines and mini-skirts that she could only wear in private.

It is not surprising that her clothes suggested a somewhat confused identity. To her sisters and friends, Diana frequently spoke of herself as two people, for example when she talked of her reaction to her sister-in-law's popularity: 'Suddenly everybody said "Oh, isn't Fergie marvellous, a breath of fresh air, thank God she's more fun than Diana." So Diana was listening and reading every line. I felt terribly insecure.'

While the press pursued the red herring of a princess rebelling against the boredom of life with a man older than his years, the truth was that despite her beauty and charm, Charles remained aloof and uninterested. Faced with the cooling of a fairy-tale marriage into a cynical arrangement, the Princess did the worst thing possible. In her attempts to recapture her husband's attention, she used ploys that would have succeeded in a romantic novel, asserting herself as provocatively. As always, her clothes played their part.

At the wedding dance of the Marquess of Worcester, she spent the evening dancing with old Etonian banker Philip Dunne, and continued to do so long after Charles had left. She went to a movie with David Waterhouse, and after a dinner party they scuffled in the street like children. 'She only wanted to have some fun,' says Jasper Conran. 'She was in her dancing years. Charles was past them — if he had ever had any. All she had ever known was boarding school and the country, and now she found herself in the heart of the city — shops, parties — married to a man she was still mad about, wealthy, at the peak of social life: and contrary to all expectations, life was no fun.'

She lacked romance and danger lay in the fact that she might find it. 'If she does,' said the *Sunday Times* in 1987 'it will be in the form of one of the attractive and entertaining men for whom her friends ransack London when she's coming to dinner. Somewhere, in some Filofax on a chintz-draped table in Pimlico or Chelsea, are the name and telephone number of the man who may one day throw the Palace into a frenzy of anxious activity.' When that

opposite Diana always looked for a way to incorporate into her dress some reference that made it appropriate to the time and place because it would be recognized that she had taken trouble. For this visit to the naval base in La Spezia, Italy, in 1985, she wore an American sailor's 'doughboy' to inspect a submarine. The hat was made by the talented milliner Graham Smith, who had already made one in organza for Princess Margaret. Diana wore it with a striped suit by Catherine Walker. Graham Smith did not know where Diana was going to wear his hat, and thought the sailor theme was mere coincidence.

below The puffball skirt was a fashion favourite in 1987, but hardly appropriate for a princess on official business. As if she lacked confidence in the look Diana teamed the padded skirt of her Catherine Walker striped dress rather oddly with a double-breasted blazer. She is pictured here in Cannes in 1987.

left Puff sleeves, handbag, necklace, John Boyd hat with band, turned-up brim and feather trim – Diana in 1985 needed to cut down on accessories.

was written, she had already met Captain James Hewitt, a handsome young polo player who was always ready to amuse her beloved boys. Predictably, his admiration and her isolation resulted in a full-blown love affair. It was conducted in two phases: from 1986 to 1987 and then from 1990 to 1991. Hewitt was – and is – a vain man, keenly aware of his good looks and appearance in general. For a while, Diana chose her clothes with him in mind, and then she chose his clothes too. As she said later, 'I dressed him from head to foot.'

As always, it was the designers who first picked up on signals that would have been invisible to most people. 'There were these little messages!' Jasper Conran recalls. 'There was a certain maturing. She became a woman rather than a girl.' From flat Manolo pumps and sensible Ferragamos that would stop her from towering over her husband, she began to wear high heels, going to Jimmy Choo for the new 2½ inch heels. When buying clothes for her private life, she had been collecting jackets or blazers with fluid pleated skirts suitable for Highgrove and nursery life. She still bought these clothes, but now she was also buying sexy and revealing evening dresses.

When she called at the showroom of Rifat Ozbek, the most colourful and exotic new name on the fashion block, he provided the strong cup of black coffee that she asked for 'because I have had a late night', and proceeded to show her his collection. He shuffled through the samples, not knowing what to show her, until she put down her coffee cup and told him, 'What I've really come for is the red dress.' This low-cut, tight mini-dress, which she had seen in *Vogue*, was the big hit of his collection and was also bought by Jerry Hall, wife of Mick Jagger, and Marie Helvin, former wife of David Bailey.

'It was a naughty, sexy dress,' says Ozbek. 'I didn't see how she would be able to wear it, and I said so. She told me "Don't worry about that. I can wear it at home, with my girlfriends." ' In fact, Diana now had few girlfriends. She said that inviting her old friends round would have been too much for her to handle, adding rather mysteriously, 'I would be apologizing the whole way through lunch.'

Diana knew that she couldn't wear dresses like that in public. She told Bruce Oldfield, a designer with a reputation for dressing movie stars and top models, 'I would love to wear a dress that was slashed to the waist, but it isn't for me!' Oldfield is a charming and persuasive character. On one occasion, when he wanted her to wear a tiny dress with a very short skirt, he looked out a photograph of Princess Margaret in the sixties in an attempt to show that such skirts were not unknown in the royal family. 'She laughed,' he says. 'She told me, "Perhaps back in the sixties Princess Margaret didn't have the paparazzi kneeling on the pavement ready to take a picture every time the car door was opened!" '

Learning from every fashion success and failure, Diana worked at her own agenda of communication with the public. She wanted to look new and different from the royal family. 'She had found out the royal rules the hard way,' says David Sassoon. 'Now she began to break the rules.' She wanted each outfit to make an impact, and her experiments were nothing if not bold. The Princess was the first royal to be photographed wearing trousers in the evening, teaming them with various tuxedo jackets. She tried wearing one long red evening glove, and one black. She tried out coloured or novelty tights, even with formal evening dresses. In 1985, she attracted criticism for wearing a wrap-over gown cut just like a dressing gown. It had a quilted collar and cuffs and a tasselled cord belt. She was to have worn it with the accompanying

below Diana knew she could not wear revealing dresses in public, but she liked to experiment with new fashions on less formal occasions. She wore the androgynous white tuxedo and bow tie on the Italian tour of 1985, and for a Genesis rock concert the same year. She is pictured here in a suit by Margaret Howell.

left Though she had the most
fabulous jewels in the world,
Diana liked to wear fashionable
costume jewellery and watch
people trying to work out if it
was the real thing. Here, with
the printed silk, waisted suit by
Bruce Oldfield that she wore
in Milan; she chose fake
earrings by Butler and Wilson.

satin trousers, but was rumoured to have lost her nerve at the last moment. Even without these, and with an evening bag and a bouffant hairdo, it still looked as if she had called in to the reception on her way to bed.

In a doubtful but eye-catching venture, she dressed Harry in a lookalike child's copy of her own pale-blue, double-breasted and braided coat, which she wore with a stock of Charles' tied in the neckline under a large Somerville hat. She had suggested the idea to the milliner when they chose the shape of the hat together. 'Oh, poor kid!' was his instinctive response, which made her roar with laughter. Later, she sent him a photograph. 'Don't worry' she teased him, 'I'll have them both in this next year!'

In her desire to project herself memorably she often went a fraction too far. There was something theatrical about some of her fashion choices. To the Christmas service at Windsor Castle in 1986, for instance, she wore a scarlet Cossack outfit. Had it snowed, she would have made a perfect subject for a Christmas card. Caped, hatted, booted and with a muff, she was a pretty sight, but she had gone beyond fashion. She was in costume, and it is but a short step from costume to pantomime. When Diana and Charles went to Gatwick Airport to greet King Fahd, she wore a gold frogged suit like a

opposite Meeting King Fahd at
Gatwick Airport, Diana went
a step too far in Catherine
Walker's white suit with drum
majorette gold frogging and
epaulettes. The press deemed
the suit pure fancy dress. The
hat in white to match was by
Graham Smith at Kangol.

drum majorette's, and the press wrote that she looked like a cut-out from the cover of the Beatles' 'Sergeant Pepper' album.

The perceptive young hat-maker Stephen Jones, who used to hand embroider the inside of her berets with her initials and the Prince of Wales feathers, studied her appearance with fascination. 'As a milliner you're aware that when someone puts a hat with an outfit it turns it into costume,' he says. 'It adds drama, status and theatricality, and the person behaves a little differently. When I met the Princess at Kensington Palace she was always interested in the effect – "How will people see this? How will it be interpreted?"'

Branching out, Diana chose by herself all the clothes she wore on the Italian tour in May 1985. With huge tricorne hats and exaggerated outlines, her wardrobe was something of a fashion disaster, but it did not send her running

above For Christmases at Windsor Castle, Diana tended to like a theatrical look that sometimes came close to costume. In 1986, with a bright military Piero de Monzi coat, she completed the Russian mood of the Marina Killery hat by adding a muff.

left and opposite Her first Jacques Azagury dress, worn in Florence in 1985, was one she had noticed on his stall at the London Designer Collections that year. Three weeks afterwards, she came to his shop in Knightsbridge and bought it. With blue stars embroidered on a long fitted black bodice, it had a bright blue organza skirt tied on the hip with a bow. She wore it in Toronto in 1986 and bought many evening dresses from Azagury up to the time of her death.

below At Easter in 1987, Diana dressed Harry in a lookalike pale blue coat, prompting some criticism, which Diana laughed off. The braided, tailored coat was by Catherine Walker, with a hunting stock belonging to Charles tied in the neckline.

back to *Vogue*. She wanted purpose and gravitas in her life, and she knew that the occasional unflattering outfit did her less harm than being defined as a clothes horse.

'She set out to win back the public through her frocks,' says Oldfield. 'She had the power, but up until now she hadn't had the persona.'

She derived her style from a handful of sources, beginning with her own press cuttings. She learnt that clothes that looked fine in the mirror did not always work in the camera lens. She studied herself from every angle. She trawled through the fashion magazines, ripping out pages and ringing Anna Harvey for the occasional introduction. She loved movies, and went to the local cinema in the afternoons, catching up on the films whose premières she hadn't attended. Disguised in a scarf and glasses, she dived from her car into the dark theatre, and back into the waiting car as she re-emerged into the daylight. She traced the milliner Philip Somerville from a hat she had spotted in a television commercial, making contact through her hairdresser, Richard Dalton. Somerville was to make some of her most spectacular hats and persuaded the Princess to wear bigger, more graphic shapes with a cleaner line. 'I explained that if you made the hat too small, the padded shoulders would look too big.'

Of all the movie stars she liked, Grace Kelly was the most real to her. She had met Princess Grace of Monaco just before her own wedding in 1981 and they had had an instant rapport. When Grace had died, Diana had asked the Queen's permission to attend the funeral. She was acutely aware of the parallels between them, even if Prince Rainier's principality was no larger than a small country town. Both were tall, blonde beauties who had married European princes and outshone them. When she attended the Cannes Film Festival in 1987, she chose a cool, classical dress by Catherine Walker, similar to the one Grace Kelly had worn in the crucial scene of Hitchcock's movie *To Catch a Thief* – a column of finely draped ice-blue chiffon with a drifting stole – and fabulous sapphire earrings. The press missed the significance of her choice.

Searching for a persona, Diana was determined to be modern.

Women in the eighties had jobs, power suits, shoulder pads and briefcases. They went to the gym three times a week, and in the evening they dressed for maximum exposure, baring their legs and backs. Diana wanted to look as up-to-date as a Princess could. Bruce Oldfield, who had grown up in a Dr Barnardo's children's home, gave Diana contemporary glamour in the *Dynasty* era. The strong, womanly look that was the theme of the decade was his particular fashion territory. Between 1986 and 1989, he provided her with many of her most regal 'function' dresses. He made the regal blue, crushed-velvet dress, with a cowl around the shoulders and a sweeping train from the hips, that she wore during an official visit to Portugal. He wanted to frame her shoulders with a band of mink, but she did not want to wear fur: it was also something the press would focus on. But the dress everyone remembers is the low-backed gold pleated lamé dress with big shoulders that she wore for the 1985 Dr Barnardo's Ball. It could have been designed for another of his customers, the *Dynasty* star herself, Joan Collins. In Oldfield's own words it was a 'flashy frock'.

above In Portugal in 1987, Diana looked as regal as she could in this royal purple velvet gown with a cowl neck and train from the waist. The designer, Bruce Oldfield, wanted to put a mink band around the shoulders, but Diana did not want to wear fur.

Diana had a healthy respect for Joan Collins and wanted a similarly strong, womanly look. Under fire from the press, she needed to dress for confidence – a confidence she didn't always feel. 'One thing the Princess always wanted was to look feminine,' says Philip Somerville. 'She said once that she had a lot of respect for Joan Collins because she always looked feminine. That didn't mean soft.'

Somerville also made hats for the *Dynasty* star, and remembers one awkward afternoon when a last minute call from Diana's butler, Paul Burrell, required him to be at Kensington Palace just as Joan Collins was due to arrive for a long-standing appointment. 'I asked the Palace if they would forgive me if I came a little later. Paul Burrell talked to the Princess and came back to the phone. He said "The Princess says that Miss Collins must certainly be seen first!"'

Physically, Diana was stronger. She tried various kinds of therapies and counselling, and by 1987 she had conquered her eating disorder. On an impulse, she had had her hair cropped into a sharper platinum bob by hairdresser Sam McKnight. Her posture was much better and her once rounded shoulders had more shape to them. She kept fit with daily swims in the Buckingham Palace pool, and sometimes worked out with the London City Ballet, of which she was the patron. She took dance lessons in Kensington Palace and soon brought in a personal trainer to increase her stamina. Dancing was her passion, and now she wanted to show what she could do: nobody could have predicted how she would do this.

In 1985, she took to the stage of the Royal Opera House, Covent Garden, and joined the famous dancer Wayne Sleep in a four-minute performance to the Billy Joel song 'Uptown Girl'. She had spent most of the evening in the royal box by her husband's side, but had slipped out, put on a dance dress of skimpy satin, and reappeared on stage. The audience kept the two dancers bowing for eight curtain calls, but in private, Prince Charles expressed his strong disapproval of her behaviour. Diana hadn't finished yet. At the end of that year, at a State Dinner at the White House given by President and Mrs Reagan, she enslaved all of America, if not her husband, by dancing with John Travolta. She was wearing one of her all-time favourite dresses, a ravishing evening dress of ink blue velvet by Victor Edelstein, cut with an Edwardian bustle and bare shoulders. She wore it with her famous sapphire-and-pearl choker and matching earrings. 'Princess Diana swept Washington's high society off its feet with a dazzling display of "Saturday Night Fever,"' said Monday's *Daily Mail*. 'In a scene more sensational than any in the disco dance movie, Travolta spun his royal partner around the marbled entrance hall of the White House to the beat of his own hit single, "You're the One That I Want."' To questions from reporters,

below If Diana was going to make a mistake, it was usually when she was trying too hard to make an impact, and impress the fashion journalists. One of her less happy clothes choices was this red and blue striped gown with cord details, worn for the start of London Fashion Week in 1985. At the last moment Diana changed her mind about wearing the blue silk pyjama pants designed to go with it but the wrapover coat still looked exactly like a dressing gown.

Prince Charles commented tersely, 'My wife would be an idiot if she didn't enjoy dancing with John Travolta.'

She was provocative and exhibitionist in public, lonely and tearful in private. As usual, the designers felt protective. 'Kensington Palace was always so quiet,' remembers Philip Somerville, who would bring boxes of hat shapes and samples with the help of his assistant, Dylan. 'When we were shown in, the Princess was always waiting to greet us at the top of the stairs. When we left she would walk us back to our car, and sometimes, if the boys were with her, they would jump in and pretend to drive.

'One year they had been given small camouflage suits, like soldiers. They lined up by the gate and saluted us as we drove by. We looked back and saw Diana standing there, and oddly enough it occurred to us that we were brightening up her day.'

In 1987, when the Waleses paid an official visit to Portugal, it was noted that they occupied separate suites. It was a watershed. Diana now confronted the three years of experimentation and came to a conclusion. Addressing herself in the third person, as usual, she said 'You've got to understand that you can't do what other 26 and 27 year olds are doing...you must adapt to the position and stop fighting it.'

Now she had the power and the persona.

above At the Reagan White House State Dinner, Diana enchanted America by taking the floor with John Travolta as the band played 'You're the One that I Want'. Inspired by an Edwardian dinner dress, the Victor Edelstein design was one of Diana's favourite evening dresses. She wore it with her trademark pearl-and-sapphire choker.

Jewel in the Crown

'When she discovered Catherine Walker, the Princess found what she needed,' says Jasper Conran, 'a designer who would design for her and concentrate on her.' The Frenchwoman was to provide the great majority of Diana's most photographed clothes over the next fifteen years. She learnt exactly what the Princess needed and was, perhaps, the last in a great tradition of royal dressmakers.

Diana had always been careful to share her custom between the talented London designers. Now, for the first time, she chiefly focused on one designer of exceptional technical skill. Catherine Walker was to provide fifteen years of absolutely devoted service, until she was forced by ill health to take a step back. She did not make all of Diana's clothes during this period, but she made by far the most important part of her public wardrobe. Crucially, Diana depended on her for the spectacular but dignified wardrobe of state for some twenty official foreign tours that she undertook with, and without, Prince Charles.

Catherine (pronounced 'Catreen') is an intense, reclusive French woman with a doctorate in aesthetics and an informed interest in social history and art. Traumatized by the death of her husband in 1975, she was eager to bury herself in work. She painstakingly taught herself tailoring and dressmaking, and by 1977, when she started The Chelsea Design Company, she was an expert pattern cutter, fitter and seamstress. The two women met for the first time after the designer had supplied her with a number of maternity dresses, through the auspices of *Vogue*.

Diana, as she came to rely on the designer for all kinds of support, recognized that their meeting was a milestone in her life. Here was a skilled and selfless designer who was prepared to put the Princess first, and had an intuitive as well as an intellectual grasp of what Diana was about. Early on, Catherine Walker showed that she was aware of both the privilege and the responsibility entailed in dressing the Princess. She soon began to fit together the trinity of aspects that the public Diana had to symbolize: future Queen, mother of the future King and ambassador for Britain. In doing so, the designer prefigured the star that Diana was becoming in her own right.

With education and interests wider than those strictly necessary for a career in fashion, it was immediately obvious to Catherine that Diana was sending signals to her public through her appearance. This mode of communication had a historical precedent, royal figures have always advertised their power and

left For a trip to Japan in 1986, Diana made a diplomatic choice – an off-the-peg dress from Tatters printed with red polka dots, or 'rising suns'. She wore it with a red straw hat to match by Frederick Fox. 'On this particular trip, she was getting in and out of cars all day,' said the milliner. 'This was the biggest brim she could manage.'

majesty through their dress. In later years, Catherine would find new ways for the Princess to win sympathy and support through her choice of clothes, but during the eighties her job was to give Diana a radiant mystique which she could then dispel with her warmth and personal approach. It was a perfect and charming combination of effects: the dress said, 'Here is the future Queen' and, at the same time, Diana's receptive, friendly manner said, 'I am delighted to meet you because you matter to me.'

In other ways, too, the designer was the perfect partner for the production of the 'Diana' image, the exciting and demanding mission in which they collaborated equally. As an outsider in London, Walker distanced herself from designer rivalry and fashion politics. She was discreet, and interested only in polishing the trophy that Diana had become. She did not have to be original, or even very fashion conscious, to suit Diana, whose position prevented her from wearing the extreme looks that were currently raising the blood pressure on catwalks in Paris and New York.

opposite Diana is pictured here on an official visit to Germany in 1987, in one of Victor Edelstein's beautiful evening dresses. Fine black lace is layered over magenta silk for richness and movement. The skirt ended in three deep lace flounces.

above For a visit to Berlin in 1987, Diana wore this coat, by German designer Escada, in blanket checks and a turban hat by Philip Somerville. When she wore the coat again, later that year, she changed the belt for one of her own.

Diana needed to learn what kind of businesses could handle her requests. Much as they coveted Diana as a customer, many of her designers were scared by the quality and quantity of what she was beginning to require. Several of the designers use the same words to describe their position: if they had put all their 'eggs in one basket' and the Princess had proved fickle, they could have found themselves bankrupt. When a call came through from Kensington Palace to ask for a quantity of outfits for an official visit, the designer could find himself in a quandary.

'Patterns had to be made specially for the Princess, and there were many fittings per dress,' explains Jasper Conran. 'Mine is a ready-to-wear company but I would do a couture job for her. I actually made a loss on each garment she ordered.'

When he was asked to provide thirty-two outfits for a certain foreign visit, he felt he had to clarify his position to the Princess herself. 'I asked to speak to her, and I said, 'Please Ma'am, don't do this to me!' I explained that if I made those thirty-two outfits, my workroom would be swamped and I wouldn't be able to produce a collection that season. I simply didn't have the resources. Once I had explained it, she was understanding.'

Catherine Walker's company could cope, although the regular customers became increasingly aware that they were no longer the designer's prime commitment. The Chelsea Design Company occupies the slot between ready-to-wear and Paris couture. Clothes are made to measure. The shop contains samples from which orders are made. Customers call in, try the outfits on, then come back for fittings for the wedding dress, suit or evening dress that they have chosen. In the sales, samples are sold off to make way for new ones. The designer of a business like this has the freedom to concentrate on a particular customer, because she does not have to supply mass orders to a list of stockists or produce a seasonal collection which lays down a trademark 'look'. Nor is she obliged to produce unwearable catwalk shockers to sell a perfume. As Catherine gradually became an integral part of Diana's support system, she did increase her production of unique dresses in answer to the Princess's unique needs.

Diana's public engagements had been building ever since the birth of Harry, and she may have felt a degree of panic at the sheer number of clothes she needed. Buying occasional outfits no longer sufficed.

On her first trip on her own, to Vienna in 1986, Diana made a spectacular appearance in Walker's mermaid dress of deep-green paillettes, worn with the fabulous emerald-and-diamond choker that she had made famous when she had worn it as a headband to dance with Prince Charles in Australia. The sequined dress was slit to the knee, and as she was without Charles, the Princess took the opportunity to wear green satin shoes with very high heels. In fact she wore Catherine Walker designs throughout the trip, but the press did not know it because the designer never spoke to journalists.

By the latter half of the eighties the foreign tours, the most demanding part of her royal duties, were beginning to be spaced at six monthly intervals. These official visits, usually undertaken together with the Prince of Wales, were meticulously planned four or five months ahead, as soon as an outline of events could be produced. First, a private secretary or press chief would fly to the host country to make what they always called a 'recce'. They would walk along routes and check buildings, writing a detailed report for their return. The report would include every detail that could have a bearing on the Prince and Princess's clothes. Along with obvious information – national colours, for instance, or reminders that women are expected to cover their bodies and veil their hair in Muslim countries

below On a visit to Saudi Arabia in November 1986, Diana looks regal in this formal black and white satin dress tying on one hip in a striped bow. The magazine *Vanity Fair* commented on the pressures she appeared to be under, saying she was, 'constrained in elegant formality at a Saudi Arabian royal banquet'.

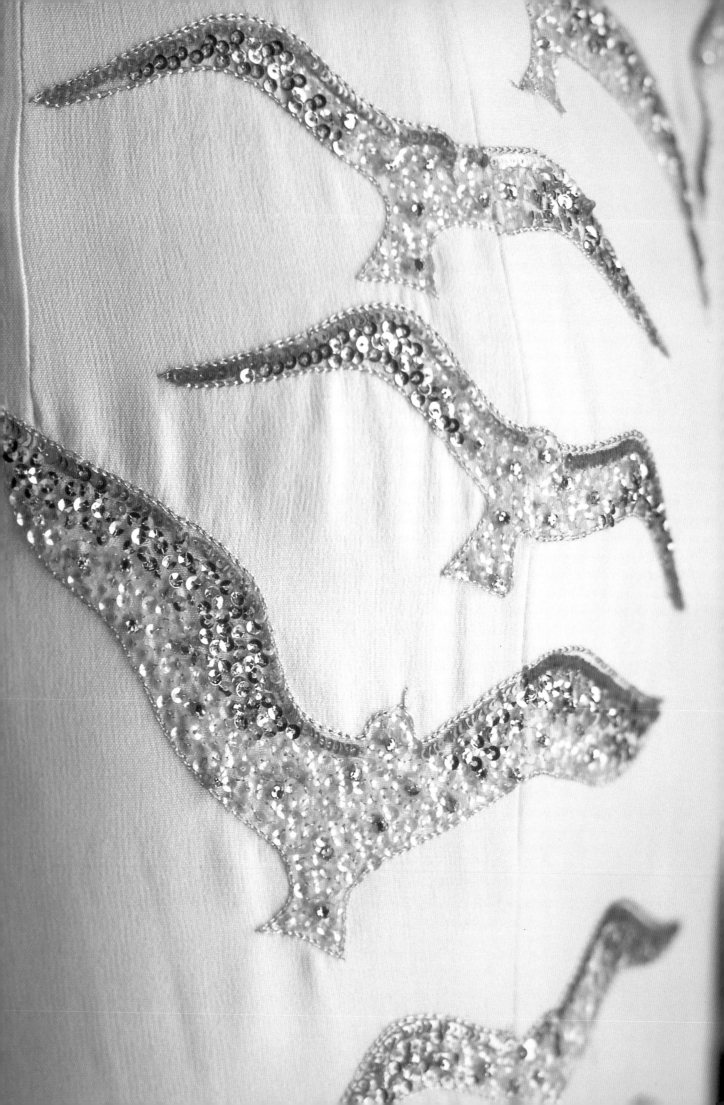

opposite Detail of the Catherine Walker dress that Diana wore to a private dinner on the visit to Saudi Arabia in 1986. The falcons were a compliment to the ruling house, and Catherine Walker embroidered a flight of them in silver and gold sequins across the bodice and down the train of a simple dress in cream silk crepe. The dress had a decorously high neckline and long sleeves, in order to conform to local custom. The embroidery was applied after the dress was made so that the bird silhouettes could flow uninterrupted by the seams.

– it might note steep stairs, or slippery cobblestones, the quantities of mud or mosquitos likely to be encountered on a country walk, or the likelihood of the Princess being faced with a crowd of style-conscious adolescents looking for fashion leads. The reports forewarned of customs such as sitting cross-legged in an Arab tent.

When the clothes were packed into the coffin-like metal wardrobe trunks, and put together with the pyramid of bags and cases by the door, each handle was tied with a colour-coded label printed 'The Princess of Wales' and carefully numbered so that the dresser with the clipboard would know where to find everything. Diana's label colour was always pink. For an important or prolonged visit, the retinue of aides grew to ten or twelve and could include two policemen, or protection officers; a private secretary; a lady-in-waiting; a

above left This ivory dress with diamanté sparkles across the bodice, which is gathered into a fan on the shoulder is from Diana's 'Dynasty' fashion phase. Designed by David and Elizabeth Emanuel, she wore this to Bahrain in 1986 with the Spencer tiara. The dress was an early variation on the asymmetric dresses that she was to wear in the late eighties.

below, right and opposite Diana
wore this printed silk taffeta
dress, by Catherine Walker,
in Melbourne, Australia in
1988. Photographs of Diana
and Charles appeared in
newspapers all over the world,
and her new hairstyle – a French
pleat – caused much comment.

press secretary; one or two dressers (usually including the invaluable Evelyn
Dagley) to press clothes, sew on buttons and produce the outfit complete with
its jewellery, tights, and accessories; a hairdresser and a baggage master.

There were occasional grumblings in the press about the money that Diana
was supposed to have spent on these travelling wardrobes. *The Times* estimated
the price of her clothes for a sixteen-day tour at £80,000: 'Even allowing for
a change of clothing every day on the sixteen-day trip,' wrote journalist Sue
Cameron, 'the cost to the taxpayer worked out at £2500 per outfit.' In fact,
Diana seldom undertook less than four separate events in a day, which suggests
that £1250 per outfit might be a more realistic average figure. The evening
dresses were bound to be expensive, but Diana liked to mix in ready-to-wear
shirts and skirts where they suited the event, just as she mixed her real jewels
with fakes to keep her audience guessing.

When Diana was going to meet the Pope in 1985, she played it safe by
wearing a full-length black lace dress with a veil by Catherine Walker. There
were echoes in her appearance of the time when Jackie Kennedy made a trip

above, right and opposite For
Thailand in 1988, Catherine
Walker's sari-style evening
dress combined the hot,
sweet colours of tropical
orchids and bougainvillaea
– flowers which Diana wore
pinned in her hair. The violet
scarf forms a single shoulder
strap and falls to the floor.

to visit Pope John XXIII in 1962. She had worn a similar long black dress with sleeves and mantilla. Catherine Walker's clothes for the Princess came to the forefront during the tour of the Gulf States in March 1989. In Saudi Arabia the Princess wore her skirts to the calf or longer, and covered her chest and arms. As a compliment to the ruling house, no less than to the middle eastern love of embroidery, Diana wore Catherine's long-sleeved white crêpe evening dress encrusted with the silhouettes of flying falcons in silver and gold sequins. The dress had been made before the embroidery was applied, and as a result the falcons flew around the bodice and over the seams without a break. For a desert picnic, Catherine made Diana a blue printed tunic with white silk trousers – a Londoner's *shalwar kameez* – in which the Princess posed cross-legged for photographs among embroidered cushions in a precisely matching colour.

Philip Somerville, one of London's most original and exciting milliners, worked with Catherine Walker to provide the hats for her outfits. For Diana, hats were pure fun. So pleased was she with his work that one day in 1987 she turned up unannounced at his shop with William, to present a thank-you letter and a bottle of champagne. In return, Somerville credits the Princess with putting hats back on the fashion map.

Walker would send the latest sketches and swatches, and the milliner would run up the plain straw 'shapes' for Diana to try on with the dresses and suits.

Before her trip to Dubai, he was reminded that women there were expected to cover their hair. She was to wear a white dress and jacket with blue revers and cuffs. When he gave her the tightly draped blue turban rather like a swimming cap, Diana doubtfully but obediently tucked all her hair inside it. With a flourish, Somerville then produced an enormous white straw brim which fitted over the turban like a tilted halo, and Diana's dubious expression gave way to a smile of pleasure.

He was equally inventive when he was asked to provide something for her to wear with an ice-blue sheath for Emperor Akihito's enthronement. 'She asked for some sort of head covering that would not give her extra height. She was worried about towering over the Japanese men she was going to meet.' He made a simple blue band which circled the crown of her head, and attached a wisp of blue veil through which Diana's eyes sparkled sapphire blue. He also made her a cream pillbox hat with one red button on the side, to symbolize Japan's rising sun.

Diplomatic dressing must be appropriate, and Diana always considered wearing at least one outfit by an easily recognized designer from the country she was visiting. For example she wore a red Chanel suit on her visit to Paris, and a checked Escada coat to visit Germany. When she went to Japan in 1986, the British designer Yuki waited hopefully for a call, but none came. Yuki was born in Japan, where he is a well known figure

below and opposite Diana wore this Catherine Walker dress several times and is pictured here at a dinner at the Château de Chambord, France. The narrow single-breasted coat dress in scalloped white lace is embroidered with blue silk and frosted white sequins.

above On her arrival in Paris in 1988, Diana diplomatically wore a scarlet Chanel suit accompanied by the trademark quilted Chanel handbag. The suit was elegant but some people criticised the choice of hat and said the outfit looked too much like an air hostess' uniform.

above and right In contrast to
the white evening dresses that
Diana chiefly wore in Paris, she
took the French by surprise with
this crimson rose and black
silk taffeta dress by Catherine
Walker, with a ruched
bodice and single sleeve.

and a very popular designer. He was embarrassed when his friends in London
and Tokyo assumed that he would be providing some of the Princess's wardrobe
for the trip.

He timidly mentioned this to a friend, the late Lord Drogheda, whose
concert-pianist wife Yuki already dressed. Garrett Drogheda's house was near
to Windsor Castle and he regularly attended the church for Sunday service.
When he happened to meet the Princess after church, he asked, 'Did you get
a letter from my old friend Yuki?' When she shook her head, he explained
the situation, adding, 'It might give a lot of pleasure if you wore one of his
dresses.' A day later, the lady-in-waiting phoned Yuki to invite him to submit
sketches. She reminded him that it was only a fortnight to departure time,
and asked whether, if the Princess chose a dress, he could complete the garment
in time. Yuki had already hopefully prepared three dresses for the Princess,
making them to measurements he had coaxed from another designer.

The Princess liked all three drawings, and Yuki took the dresses to
Kensington Palace immediately, where he found Diana playing the background

opposite Milliner Philip Somerville
knew that Diana liked her fringe
to show beneath her hats, but
needed to follow Dubai custom
by covering her hair on the
official visit in 1986. He
presented her with a blue
turban which she reluctantly
tucked her hair into. He than
produced the large white halo
brim and she was delighted
with the result. She wore the
hat with a blue and white
Catherine Walker suit.

H.R.H. The Princess of Wales

1986

opposite, right and above Diana wore this Yuki dress for a banquet with Emperor Hirohito in Japan, 1986. Inspired by Fortuny pleating and the designs of Erte, it was beaded around the yoke and at the waist. The Princess wore it with her sapphire headband, a look that was taken up briefly by the fashion press.

music of a favourite movie, *The Mission*. 'They fitted perfectly, and when she asked how I knew her measurements, I told her that I had a spy.'

As it happened, Yuki was in Japan for his licensee business when the Prince and Princess arrived. When day after day passed without the Princess wearing his dresses, he felt he had lost face. Then, at the last moment and for the highlight of the visit, the banquet with Emperor Hirohito, Diana wore a hallmark dress of Yuki's: an uncrushable royal-blue dress of Fortuny pleats, with bugle-bead panels at the neck and waist. She was still wearing it when she boarded the Queen's Flight to go home that night.

Diana's patronage raised Yuki's profile in both countries. Like other designers before him, he wanted to thank her by 'forgetting' to send the bill, but he was not allowed to. The palace insisted, and the bill was paid.

The supreme test of Diana's fashion life came in November 1988, when she went on an official visit to Paris. For the princess, it was a real-life version of the ball at which *Pygmalion*'s Eliza Doolittle runs the gauntlet of high society:

in Diana's case it was the critical moment by which she would always be judged
by the fashion critics. There was ample reason for her to be nervous in the
birthplace of haute couture and the home of the cruellest sartorial critics on
earth. British royalty had received extremely mixed reactions in Paris since
Queen Victoria, on a state visit, had been mocked for her dusty travelling
bonnet and her handbag crudely embroidered with a poodle. In choosing a
wardrobe of predominantly white dresses, Diana surely had in mind the
triumphant state visit of George V1 and Queen Elizabeth, the Queen Mother,
in the summer of 1938. The couturier Norman Hartnell had already completed
some thirty outfits for Queen Elizabeth when her mother, Lady Strathmore,
suddenly died. The trip was set back while he remade her wardrobe in white,
which has been an accepted alternative to black for royal mourning since
Queen Victoria's insistence on a white funeral. In the event, Elizabeth's filmy
white dresses, combined with her blue eyes and perfect complexion, upstaged
every couture dress in every room she entered, and when she appeared at a

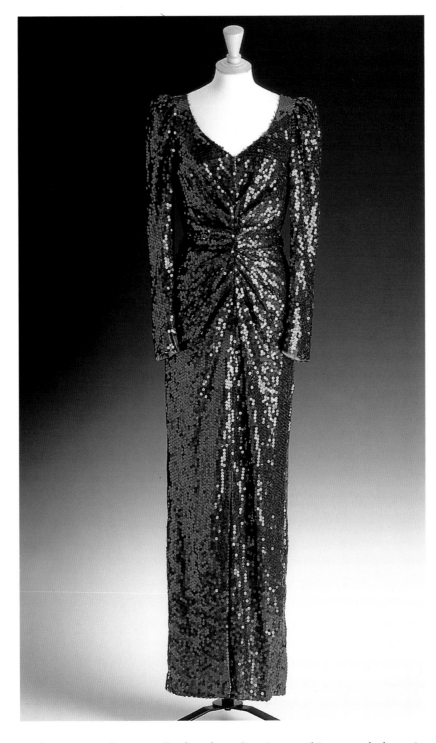

right and opposite This shimmering 'mermaid' dress by Catherine Walker was worn by the Princess in Vienna in 1986. The dress, which is slit to the knee, was embroidered all over with petrol-green sequins by Jacob Schlaepfer.

garden party at the Bagatelle, face framed against a white parasol, the train of her snowy lace dress trailing behind her across the grass, she won everyone's heart.

Diana hesitated about what to wear for the state banquet given by President and Madame Mitterand at the Elysée Palace but decided on Victor Edelstein's majestic formal dinner dress in oyster duchesse satin with a bolero jacket. The long-sleeved jacket and bodice were embroidered by the French couture craftsman Hurel with sprays of flowers and leaves worked in simulated pearls

above At the Louvre, in Paris in 1988, Diana wore a dress by Chanel. She wore several white outfits on the trip – an allusion to Queen Elizabeth the Queen Mother's all white Paris wardrobe of 1938. This striking dress has contrasting black sleeves and buttons.

and white bugle beads, finely outlined with gold beads. The skirt was pleated into a bustle back. It was a *grande toilette* as magnificent as any jewelled robe worn by Queen Elizabeth I, and it became Diana's favourite dress from her wardrobe of state. At a cost of around £55,000, it was also the most expensive dress she had ever bought. She could not have looked more beautiful or dignified, and when she came to auction her dresses in 1997 it was the one she was most reluctant to part with. For the remainder of the visit, Diana wore Catherine Walker, most notably a full-length, double-breasted coat dress of lace frosted with white sequins and threads of pale blue silk that she wore for a dinner at the Château de Chambord. With both dresses she wore the simple pearl-drop earrings given to her for a wedding present by the Emir of Qatar, and high-heeled white satin shoes.

By now Diana had been studying her image for almost a decade, in print and on camera, and she had become one of the most accomplished non-political performers on the world's stage. Her poise was unshakeable, her following worldwide. Through the medium of her charity work she had begun to reveal herself as truly committed to humanity. She was the mistress of a rewarding symbiosis. She used her work, and her work used her. She was a force to be reckoned with, and acutely aware of herself as a star. She was about to become the greatest media personality on the map.

opposite Diana's blue headband with a wisp of veil was Philip Somerville's response to her request for a hat that would not add to her height. She was worried that she would tower over the Japanese people when she visited Tokyo in 1990 for the enthronement ceremony of Emperor Akihito. She wore a pale-blue sheath by Catherine Walker.

right and below When, from time
to time, Diana had to wear
uniform or protective clothing,
she still managed to retain her
beauty and charm. Just as the
fashion designers agreed that it
was impossible to make Diana
look vulgar, it was also
impossible to make her look
unfeminine.

opposite On a visit to the
13th/18th Royal Hussars
regiment in June 1988, Diana
wears army 'denims' – which
were made specially for her
visit – to climb aboard a tank.

New Testament

In the late eighties, Diana had been dressing for Britain. In the nineties, dressing down became as important a part of her diplomatic armoury as dressing up. Through her clothes she appealed for understanding from the public as she dealt the monarchy its worst blow since the abdication of Edward VIII.

1992 was the year the Queen referred to as her 'annus horribilis', the year Diana exposed the truth about her marriage through Andrew Morton's book, the year the disgraced Fergie separated from Prince Andrew, the year of the Wales' official separation and the year of the 'Squidgygate' tapes. For these reasons and others, they were horrible years for Diana, too. She was suffering from empty nest syndrome after the start of the school year in 1991, when both boys went to boarding school. The following year her father died.

Diana: Her True Story revealed, in author Andrew Morton's own words, 'a life totally at variance with the accepted image'. Speaking into an old tape recorder and prompted by Morton's questions delivered by a third party, Diana was candid and her testimony was devastating. She let the world into the secret of her miserable marriage and the lack of understanding and care accorded her by the royal family. When the book was published in serial form in the *Sunday Times* from 7 June 1992, nine days before publication of the book, the effect on the royal family, the

opposite In July 1992, when she wore this dress to the London Coliseum, Diana had just astounded the world by aiding journalist Andrew Morton to publish the true story of her marriage. For this evening, one of the first times she had been seen in public since the book's publication, she dressed for sympathy in a Catherine Walker dress. The gentle colouring, decorous cut and flattering line, together with the fact that she was wearing an easily recognized dress that emphasized the prudent re-use of her wardrobe, proved that Diana had worked out all the angles.

previous page Diana was far from happy on this official visit with Charles to Nigeria in 1989. The soft, romantic printed silk chiffon evening dress by Catherine Walker highlighted her melancholy mood, crossing over to fasten at the nape of the neck, with a floating scarf.

establishment and the public was shattering. Diana had admitted to an eating disorder and attempts at suicide, and revealed that Prince Charles had had a mistress, Camilla Parker-Bowles, for most of the marriage. The following day the Prince and Princess met at Kensington Palace and agreed to separate. At a traumatic confrontation that followed at Windsor Castle, this decision was deferred until they had attempted a reconciliation.

Clothes were no longer Diana's main mode of communication, but they remained excellent transmitters of her mood. Besieged, solitary, sometimes despairing, she now dressed for sympathy. *Vogue* praised her more consistent style. 'The Catherine Walker suits and coat dresses say: working woman,' wrote Sarah Mower in 1991. 'The evening dresses announce: royal grandeur. The dropping-Harry-at-school clothes reassure: Kensington mother.'

above Diana takes the boys to school in her 'Kensington mother' clothes – suede blouson, print dress and flattish heels.

She had to keep on with the relentless programme of royal events, but her evening function dresses for wearing in Britain – now almost all by Catherine Walker or Victor Edelstein – were black or so dark in colour that they made her look like a tragic but elegant young widow. Abroad, for the remaining official tours Charles and Diana were obliged to make together, she dressed in fragile pastel colours that made her look demure, virginal and vulnerable.

Catherine Walker seemed possessed of a sixth sense where Diana's clothes were concerned. Now a close friend, she knew exactly how Diana was feeling and was intuitive about the mood that the Princess wanted to create. She dressed her in pale and pleasing evening dresses that no longer bared a leg or shoulder but were often long sleeved and always high-necked. She decorated them prettily with sugary embroidery and beads. For the tour of India, the beadwork resembled the border of a Moghul painting, the intricate patterns of marquetry or the pierced marble screens of the fabulous Indian palaces, each a wonderful foil for the Spencer tiara that Diana now preferred to wear. Gone were the days when Diana would encourage the designer to 'Go for it!' The Princess grew more regal as she drew further from the royal family. She was a dutiful woman and now that she was no longer seen as the traditional wife in an ideal marriage, she was doubly determined to conduct herself in public as the mother of the future

right and opposite In contrast to the 'sympathy dressing' to come, Diana wore this spectacular femme fatale dress to a première of *Dangerous Liaisons* in 1989. By the master couturier Victor Edelstein, it was a pastiche of a man's tailcoat in black velvet and ribbed silk braid, with paste buttons. Her confidence was boosted at this time and it showed in the clothes she chose to wear.

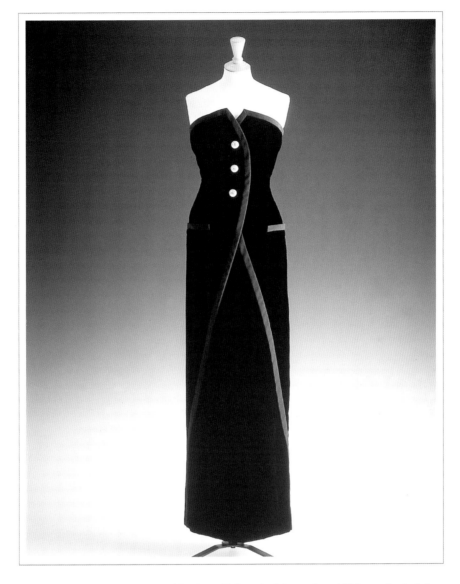

king. For a reception at Buckingham Palace in November 1992, on the brink of the official separation, Walker designed her a dress that was as traditionally royal and old fashioned as she could make it. Full skirted, of cream duchesse satin with pearl and sequin embroidery, it could almost have come from one of the Cecil Beaton portraits of the young Princesses Elizabeth and Margaret in a bower of misty white flowers. Having burnt her boats with the royal family, Diana wanted to modernize and take on the image of a nineties working woman. She threw herself into her charity work like a woman possessed, and the public woke up to the fact that in Diana they had a consummate professional in the traditional royal role of charity worker. There had never been a member of the royal family so well suited to the interface of what Diana called 'the Work': a job which she took very seriously, and in which she invested her whole psychology.

Now more than ever, Diana was more interested in image than fashion. Her wardrobe of state for public occasions and official tours was completely

right and opposite For the remaining joint official tours with Prince Charles, Diana continued to need spectacular function dresses but these were less fashionable and more conventional and colourful than before. Whereas she had worn clashing colours, slit skirts, one-shouldered dresses and looks picked up from fashion magazines and movie stars, she now wore pale dresses decorated with embroidery. As always, Catherine Walker came up with an appropriate element to the dress, one which would elicit a warm response from the country visited. Here, for the Indian tour in 1992, the beadwork resembled the border of a Moghul painting.

at odds with the navy blazers, white shirts and long dark skirts she wore for charity field work. The nineties saw her adopt the suit as her uniform: by day she almost always wore a crisp jacket buttoned over a short narrow skirt, with dark tights and shoes. When she absented herself from Royal Ascot in 1991 for three days out of five, she told friends, 'I don't like the glamorous occasions any more. I feel uncomfortable with them. I would much rather be doing something useful.'

It was not that she loved clothes any less. Like any beautiful young woman with time, money and a mantelpiece loaded with invitations to glittering events, fashion was her playground. The people around her noted that she still talked about clothes all the time, and would ask the footman, the butler, the cleaner and the driver, 'How do I look?' and, 'What do you think of this?' They soon found that a qualified answer, such as, 'It looks fine, but it's not my absolute favourite,' would put them out of favour with her all day. If she invited them

to choose between two outfits, they learnt not to commit themselves, for she would already have decided which to wear and only wanted confirmation. It was one of her most typically feminine characteristics, together with the pretence that she found dressing up an imposition: 'You men are so lucky!' She analysed other people endlessly in terms of their style, and liked to taunt men about their crumpled jackets or ancient macintoshes. At the Child of Achievement Awards in London in early 1993 she met the comedian Bill Oddie, who had turned up in his usual rumpled jacket and open-necked shirt. She laughed and teased him mercilessly, 'I see you've really dressed up for the event!'

right and opposite On the brink of the official separation, Diana attended a reception at Buckingham Palace in November 1992. Growing more regal as her status became more ambiguous, Diana worked out with Catherine Walker a dress that was so traditional it could have been made for the Queen when she was Princess Elizabeth. In cream satin with pearl and sequin embroidery, it was about fifty years out of date.

right In 1987 Diana had famously held hands with an AIDS patient for the cameras. A breakthrough gesture at the time, it did much to remove the stigma of AIDS, and to air Diana's compassion and commitment to her charities. For the occasion, opening the first ward for AIDS patients at Middlesex Hospital, Diana wore a discreet navy blue working suit by Victor Edelstein.

She needed her causes as much as her causes needed her. As Baroness Jay, daughter of the ex-prime minister Lord Callaghan, who invited the Princess to be patron of the National AIDS Trust, commented, 'If you're the product of a broken home, if you haven't been thought of as very clever, then you marry into a dysfunctional family and your husband isn't supportive, and your marriage starts to break up, then you badly need to be good at something. It's about your sense of worth and fulfilment.'

Her chosen image for the nineties was executive woman. In wanting to become a modern professional, charity work gave her a vital perspective and point of contact. She hosted a networking party at Kensington Palace, where, standing beside William and Harry, she gave a short address to say that she was looking for ways in which the charities could work together and pool their

opposite One of Diana's favourite evening dresses was Victor Edelstein's fuschia pink silk column with a draped bodice. Beautiful from all angles, the wrapover skirt, apparently about to split and reveal a leg, was a neat inverted pleat. Diana wore this dress at least eight times between 1990 and 1992, in refutation of press criticism about the money she spent on her wardrobe and upkeep.

fields of enterprise. She could put a tiny charity on the map, so that they received support from committees who had never previously heard of them, thus enabling them to fundraise on a different scale. Her presence alone could spotlight a charity's work, anywhere in the world.

Diana recognized that fashionable clothes would impede her acceptance into serious circles, and get in her way. The press office of Buckingham Palace had refused to give out her designers' names to reporters some years previously. 'The media put the emphasis on fashion and we've been working pretty hard to get the emphasis off fashion,' Dickie Arbiter, then press chief, had said. She would be seriously disappointed and annoyed to find that, after a day of hard work in which she had exhibited her emergent statesmanlike qualities, her sympathy for the underprivileged, her love of children, her diplomatic ability and her knowledge of a medical problem, the press had only written about the length of her skirt.

left For her first official foreign trip since the separation, Diana went hatless and dressed down to try and focus attention on her work. Here at the Anandaban Leprosy Mission in Nepal, she wore a pink jacket and spotted skirt by Paul Costelloe that she had had for some time. The unlined skirt proved transparent in the strong sunlight, and to her annoyance the press' attention was focused on this rather than on her programme of events.

opposite The stiffness and formality of this Snowdon portrait of the family group told its own story in 1991. Diana was scared of horses and hated riding. The message contained was one of sham and discomfort: a deliberate comment by a great photographer.

I saw this for myself on Diana's trip to Nepal to highlight the work of the British aid programme and support the Red Cross and the Leprosy Mission. The Princess entered the men's ward of the remote Anandaban Mission in a pale pink jacket over a calf-length pleated skirt. Placing her hands together in the prayer position of the traditional Nepal greeting, she greeted the patients one by one and then sat smiling on each bed, stroking each damaged limb and listening carefully as the doctor described the treatment. The patients displayed their pitiful disfigurements humbly, some of them scarcely daring to look up into her face. She touched the cheek of a man with milk white eyes whose face was undergoing surgical reconstruction, and smiled at another patient who knitted furiously for her approval. The way she touched the sick and dying was almost like an act of healing, a laying on of hands.

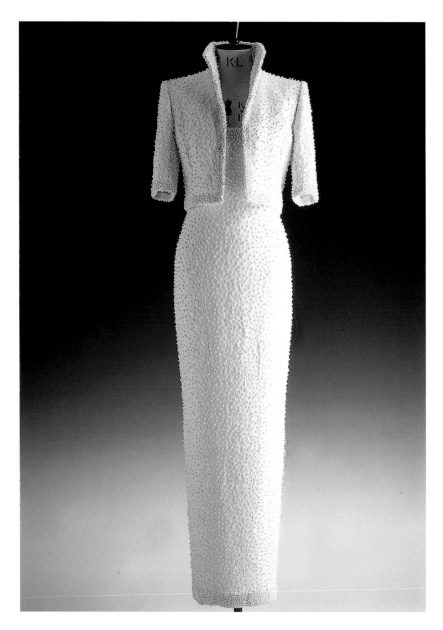

left and opposite This strapless dress and jacket in white crepe, scattered with sequins and pearls, was designed by Catherine Walker. Diana most memorably wore it to the British Fashion Awards at the Albert Hall in 1989, but it had been made for a visit to Hong Kong. She wore it with and without the jacket. It was designed as a glamorous but regal function dress, with the upstanding collar inspired by Elizabethan ruffs. Nevertheless, it came to be known as the 'Elvis dress', after Presley's white Las Vegas outfit.

The following day, she found that as usual, the tabloids preferred to dwell not on the Leprosy Mission but on the decorous but transparent skirt she had worn to visit the Ghurka regiment – 'Decidedly Diaphanous Diana' read the *Daily Mail*. 'The see-through skirt is all over the place,' reported Judy Wade of *Hello!* magazine, emerging from the fax room and addressing a knot of reporters outside. 'The lepers didn't get a look in!'

On charity visits and official trips on her own she embraced a conservative, working woman's wardrobe: clean lines, very little jewellery but special buttons, often brass, that defined the cut for the cameras and lifted the coat or suit out of the ordinary. In early 1987, wearing a discreet navy blue suit by Victor Edelstein, when she had opened the first ward for AIDS patients at the Middlesex Hospital and made the famous breakthrough gesture – courageous at the time – of holding hands with them.

When she flew in to Tokyo for a four day visit in early 1995, she took a wardrobe of beige and dark-coloured double-breasted suits from Tomasz Starzewski and Moschino. She arrived carrying a briefcase of papers, wearing a waisted navy jacket over a short skirt with a classic camel-hair coat over her shoulders. To make her speech at the National Children's Hospital – for which she had taken a four week crash course in Japanese – she wore a gently cut pale-pink suit with notched lapels and brass buttons. To visit a daycare centre for children with learning difficulties, she wore a powder-blue Louis Feraud suit with ribbon braid and blue-and-gold buttons. She wore the plainest black wool coat to visit the Commonwealth War Graves at Yokohama, and a dark blue suit with a velvet collar to meet Emperor Akihito and Empress Michiko.

right, opposite and overleaf
Catherine Walker's pale pink sarong-style dress for the official visit to Pakistan in 1991 had an appropriate paisley pattern embroidered in pearl and gold glass beads with paste sparkles. It was a perfect 'sympathy' dress which she wore on several later occasions, notably for a Royal Variety Performance which was her last public engagement before the separation.

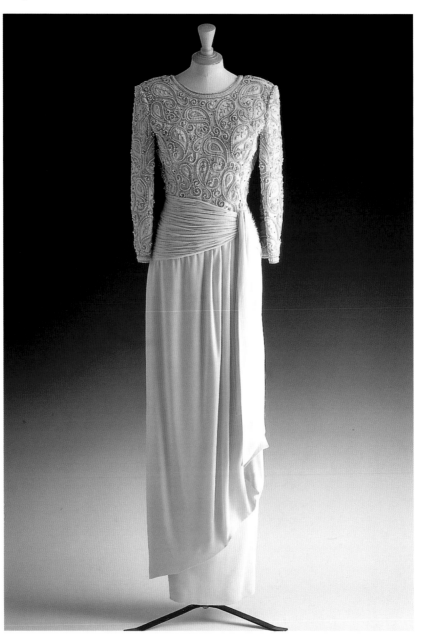

She had favourite charity outfits she wore time and again, such as the paintbox print silk dress with short sleeves that she ordered for a visit to the Save the Baby Fund in 1990. 'I called that part of her wardrobe her caring clothes,' says Sassoon. 'She said that she wanted "a cheerful dress" that children would like.' She took the dress on an official visit to Brazil in 1991, where she was photographed cuddling an HIV-positive toddler, and continued to wear it for four more years. She dressed as conscientiously for children as she did for presidents and prime ministers, generally in pastel colours and soft, 'friendly' textures with interesting buttons and jewellery that could not scratch. She wore a gold chain for babies to play with when she picked them up, to distract them from crying.

opposite Patrick Demarchelier's portrait of Diana as an independent spirit in 1992 showed the public a modern woman with a new, shorter haircut, wearing a plain black sweater. A milestone in Diana's style and development, it was used as a cover for British *Vogue*.

previous page The photograph said it all: Diana greeted her sons in a Moschino check suit with a striped ribbon slotted through the jacket. She wore the suit on a number of occasions, changing the ribbon, knowing it would be recognized that she was making the most of her wardrobe. By September 1991 she was suffering from 'empty nest syndrome'.

left Diana's jackets had special treatments from her designers by 1991: they were interlined and toughened so that they never creased. Her hair was shorter and easier to keep tidy on the charity circuit and abroad, as here, on tour in Canada.

Because her charities brought her into contact with people from all spheres of life, she turned her back on sophisticated fashion choices. She discounted, for instance, the crumpled look that became fashionable with unstructured Armani jackets and white linen, because although it might look fine on Sloane Street or Madison Avenue, it looked terrible in newspaper photographs, with every crease casting its shadow in the flashlight. The designers learned to work in a special way for her.

'For Diana, the rules were different,' says Tomasz Starzewski. 'We found fabrics for her that looked like linen, but wouldn't crumple. We would take a jacket that she liked and remount it for her, so it wouldn't get to look tired at the end of the day.' Catherine Walker made jackets for Diana that were virtually indestructable, with layers of extra padding and linings. 'It made the Princess look a little old-fashioned – you can't deny it,' says Starzewski. 'She was not directional in fashion, but she knew what worked for her.'

The Princess first met hairdresser Sam McKnight in 1991 on a *Vogue* sitting with photographer Patrick Demarchelier and Anna Harvey. Then and there he had cropped her hair into an easy modern silhouette while cosmetic artist Mary Greenwell had lightened her make up to match. By the end of the session, Demarchelier was to tell *Hello!* magazine, 'She'd changed her look, found a stylist and a hair stylist... and gained a new kind of confidence.' With her short hair and crisp looks, Diana could spend all day in a hospice or prison and look as fresh when she left as when she arrived. She never failed to take the greatest care over her appearance wherever she went. 'When she was off to some charity function I would sometimes tell her, "Your hair looks fine,"' Sam McKnight told Anna Harvey. 'She would reply "But, Sam, these people are expecting Princess Diana!"'

Keen not to seem extravagant after it was circulated that Prince Charles had complained about her £3000-a-week grooming budget, she recycled many of her clothes. The same jacket would appear with different skirts and dresses, or a long sleeved evening dress would reappear with a strapless bodice. A Moschino check suit with a red jacket and black skirt was slotted with black braid for one occasion, striped ribbon for another. The intricately embroidered bodice of a full-skirted function dress would be snipped off and fitted to a narrow sheath.

below In 1995, Diana was firmly back on the international stage, paying a goodwill visit to Japan. In her new role as modern working woman, she arrived in Tokyo in a dark suit and continued to dress in an executive woman's wardrobe of simple suits, without a single hat. Her high heels were a sign of confidence, but when curtseying to Emperor Akihito and Empress Michiko, she had almost to kneel on the floor to bring her head to their level.

To balance the new practicality of her working image, Diana had a gym-tuned figure that delighted her designers. She now held her head up and never slouched. After an experimental visit to a gym called LA Fitness in Hounslow, where a hidden camera was used to take a photograph that was sold to a tabloid newspaper, she went three times a week to the Harbour Club in Chelsea. 'Her shoulders were beautiful... wonderful,' enthuses Tomasz Starzewski. 'She carried a jacket perfectly. She had naturally square shoulders and needed only the lightest of shoulder pads.'

'Diana had cultivated a fantastic body, a beautiful silhouette and a graceful way of moving,' says the great Italian designer, Valentino, who has spent a lifetime dressing such famously good-looking women as Jackie Kennedy, Sally Aga Khan and Queen Noor of Jordan. 'She was never stiff, she always seemed relaxed, and she was a delight to dress because she gave real life to the clothes. She did not dress to be glamorous, she dressed to please. Everything she did was to please the people.'

Through the book Diana had found a great sense of release and empowerment in putting the record straight. At the same time she had dreaded its publication, and there are suggestions that she would have changed her mind about it if she had been able. Her life now changed for the worse. Prone to depression and despair, she no longer had even the support of the Duchess of York within the royal family. After a demeaning scandal, Fergie had separated from Prince Andrew in March 1992. The present fury of the Duke of Edinburgh and the hostility of the palace was wounding. She had been made to feel an outsider before, but now she witnessed the establishment closing ranks against her. Just as Diana's friends had rallied around her, supporting the story she had told, now Charles's friends informed the media that she was a sick woman with 'a hazy grasp of reality', a megalomaniac whose behaviour was endangering the future of the country. The Cambridge don John Casey predicted, 'She will be diminished, especially when she loses her youthful looks... the Princess doesn't stand for anything.' Royalist pundit Sir Peregrine Worsthorne, former editor of the *Sunday Telegraph*, predicted that the 'electric charge' between Diana and the public would now dissipate. 'I don't see her carrying on as a star in her own right, as if she's got some momentous glamour of her own.'

Conspiracy theories abounded when, two months after publication of the book, the transcript of a private conversation allegedly between the Princess and a mystery lover was published in the *Sun* newspaper. The man, who used the pet name 'Squidgy' fourteen times to address the woman, was thought to be James Gilbey, with whom the Princess had a close friendship at the end of the eighties, between her two separate affairs with James Hewitt. The scandal went down in history as 'Squidgygate' and was one of the most embarrassing

opposite The paintbox silk dress made for Diana to wear to the *Save the Baby Fund* in 1990, and many times subsequently. According to the designer, David Sassoon, Diana called it her 'caring dress'. She wore it here, in Brazil in 1991, on a day which included a visit to HIV positive babies. Diana now wanted to concentrate on charity fieldwork rather than sitting on the sidelines watching polo matches or attending formal events.

below Dressing for sympathy in 1991 and 1992, Diana had never worn so much pink and white. For the visit to Brazil she wore Catherine Walker's one-sleeved dress with shaded sequin flowers and beaded border.

episodes of Diana's life. 'I feel destroyed,' she told a friend. It would be followed by further unwelcome revelations with the publication of a distastefully intimate conversation apparently between Prince Charles and Camilla Parker-Bowles.

As the child of a broken home and a former bulimic, Diana identified certain aspects of her own predicament with the causes of her charities. As someone accused of self-absorption, attention seeking and worse, she found it easy to accept the new non-judgmental approach to drugs and irresponsible behaviour. She had a personal campaign to dispel any kind of social stigma.

Diana now found a better way to communicate than indirectly through appearance and body language, or sensationally, through a third party out of her control. She now explained herself directly to the public through the medium of the speeches she wrote herself for her charity functions, and for which she carefully prepared with lessons in voice production. At the Turning Point premiere of a movie significantly titled *Hear My Song*, she made a speech in which she said, 'Often the most disturbing feature of mental illness is just how little it takes for people... to move off their normal behaviour before they are labelled crazy or unstable. Even to understand just how trapped they can feel when in the depths of depression can help enormously.'

Early in 1992, at the Calcutta hospice of the late Mother Teresa, the nun
whose work for the poor and dying earned her the Nobel Peace Prize, Diana
prayed and wept. Stricken not to have met Mother Teresa herself, who was in
Rome undergoing treatment for a heart attack, Diana flew to the nun's side,
embraced her, and knelt with her to pray for the world's starving and destitute.
In bidding her farewell, Mother Teresa uttered the five unforgettable words
by which Diana would henceforward conduct her work, the mystical legend
for her independent coat of arms: the princess, she said, was 'doing God's work
on earth'.

But Diana had not yet renounced the world, and her desire to remake and
improve herself was the first sign of recovery. She was still the world's top
cover girl. Any magazine could raise its circulation by the use of her name on
the cover, and if, as predicted by her denigrators, the 'electric charge' between
Diana and the public was to be switched off, there was no sign of it yet. In
Nepal, the first official foreign trip since the separation, it did not escape her
sidelong look that the full complement of press was in attendance in this tiny

above Cream silk dinner dress by Catherine Walker, with yoke and sleeves of intricate ribbon and bead embroidery and a paste and pearl bead medallion. Diana wore the dress on her official solo trip to Nepal, for dinner with Crown Prince Dipendra. Once, she would have ordered a dress specially for the occasion. Now her priorities had changed and she revived a dress that had been made for her eleven years previously. She was more anxious than ever not to be seen as a fashion plate.

opposite At a charity function at the London Hilton, Diana announced her withdrawal from public life, pleading for time and space. She wore a bottle green executive suit by Amanda Wakely, with velvet lapels. Her announcement was greeted with sadness and confusion, and was taken to mean that she was abandoning the charity work that she had made her own. In fact, she was cutting down on the events that bored her so that she could concentrate on charities closest to her heart.

and remote country. Far away that afternoon, on the ski slopes of Klosters, sporting a jaunty cravat, the Prince of Wales was posing for a lone photographer. He turned to his mountain guide, Bruno Sprecher, and asked, 'Where is everyone?'

And yet the events of 1992 had been enormously damaging to Diana as well. To continue as a star of popular world culture, a priceless asset to the charities she supported, didn't she need the endorsement of royal credentials? Would she retain her royal title? Abruptly, at a charity lunch in aid of the Headway National Head Injuries Association, on 3 December 1993, she delivered a 'resignation speech', saying that the media exposure had been overwhelming, and appealing for 'time and space' to reduce the extent of the public life she had led so far. She was clearing the decks, and the world held its breath.

Sweet Revenge

In public at least, Diana never played the victim again. Employing the skills she had learnt so painfully, she became the arch manipulator of her image, using the limited means in her power to challenge Charles at every point. Behind the scenes, she was frustrated and angry. Her shrinking options left her little room for manoeuvre. Of all the transformations Diana had undergone, from kindergarten teacher to Princess to single parent, her toughest challenge was to move from a supporting royal role to a solo performer.

Polls in early 1994 revealed that Diana was still the most popular member of the royal family and after an eleven-month break she was soon back in the public eye. 'Back,' she told friends, 'with a vengeance.'

The co-operation Diana had allowed her friends to give author Andrew Morton had resulted in a book that rocked the monarchy and won the Princess massive sympathy. But the Prince's riposte, the Jonathan Dimbleby book that told Charles's side of the story, and the television interview that went with it on 29 June 1994, failed to win him the same public support. He admitted an adulterous relationship with Camilla Parker-Bowles, agonized, and soon declared that he regretted the whole exercise.

previous page The occasion was
Viscount Linley's wedding, and
Diana looked radiant in the
shortest white dress under a
dove-grey jacket trimmed with
white. The suit was by Catherine
Walker, the hat by Marina
Killery. Wearing the same
suit to the Westminster Abbey
service to mark the anniversary
of the Battle of El Alamein,
and despite the sombre
occasion, Diana wore scarlet
nail polish for the first time.

Whereas Charles had justified himself and was
now getting on with his life, Diana was caught in
limbo. While Church and State deliberated every
permutation of the constitutional implications of
divorce and possible remarriage, the thirty-
something Princess was caught in a time warp. For
any other woman, an openly acknowledged
separation would have brought more freedom. A
year or two after their separation, most women
begin to find their own concerns more interesting
than their ex-husband's. As life takes over, the urge
to compete recedes. For Diana, life could not move
on until she could identify a role for herself. She
wanted to 'do what I can do best' and carve out a niche for herself as an
ambassador for Britain, but now even her achievements were turned to her
disadvantage. The Palace blocked many of her suggested trips in case, once
again, she stole the limelight from the Prince. She wanted to set up a charitable
foundation, a companion to the Prince's Trust, but that project failed to meet
with palace approval for the same reason.

Low self-esteem had changed into an overwhelming urge to improve herself. Whatever she undertook to do, she did obsessively well. Just as she had turned to the professionals to improve her speech, taking lessons from actor Terence Stamp and voice coach Peter Settelen, so that she could communicate her message clearly and effectively through her charity pronouncements, she now used every polished public appearance to win support and prove she could do a good job for her country.

On her Washington visit, Diana met Hillary Clinton and then told a reporter, 'I hope we can now look forward to the future rather than hang onto the past.' Yet her very presence in the United States, where she was fêted by all, was calculated to detract from the Prince of Wales's visit to the States a week later. Arriving in California, he undertook his usual conscientious schedule, which included visiting an education centre for Hispanics and an inner city supermarket, but it was too late. All America had decided to take his wife's side.

Despite the pious assertion that she hoped to put the past behind her, Diana's agenda betrayed her. To be the Princess of Wales at this stage was, in the words of a U2 song, to, 'cry without weeping, talk without speaking, scream without raising your voice.' It was another demonstration that she could outshine him any time she pleased. As Diana turned again to her clothes to convey messages, the Americans coined a new phrase for her fashion, 'revenge couture'. On the day the Prince released pictures of himself tumbling on the Scottish grass with William and Harry, Diana moved onto the front pages with a sequinned, halterneck dress for a party at the Ritz. 'Glam, set and match to Di' said the tabloids. An operator of matchless skill at this game, she varied the note by taking William and Harry, aged twelve and nine, to a Catholic hostel for the homeless on the same day the Prince of Wales was photographed in top hat and morning suit at the opening of Royal Ascot. On this occasion, Diana wore jeans.

As her life closed in, she made an alternative career of her body and soul. No movie star devoted more time to fitness or grooming than Diana at this time of her life. She spent a reported £150,000 a year on her personal upkeep, and the newspapers claimed that she spent £80,000 a year on grooming expenses alone. The *Daily Mail* speculated that her wardrobe must be worth £1,000,000. Besides the beauty routines there was an army of therapists: pychiatrist, reflexologist, aromatherapist, astrologist, tarot card reader, psychic and various mystics with whom she endlessly discussed her problems. Hidden inside her clothes she wore a white crystal for a clear mind, stability and harmony. For the first time in the history of Kensington Palace, her living quarters were subjected to the oriental rites of feng shui. To her workouts and

opposite In Sydney, at a benefit dinner in October 1996, Diana wore a sliver of turquoise silk caught on one shoulder, and T-bar satin shoes to match. The dress was by her favourite designer of the moment, Versace, who had a way of making her look simply elegant and modern. The international designers described her appearance as 'minimal chic'.

fitness sessions at the Harbour Club she added a bizarre new venture. At least once a week she would attend a men's gym in London's Earls' Court, and slug away at a punchbag which she no doubt identified with the cause of her problems. Now, whatever she felt in private, she walked tall with her head up and a radiant smile, with high heels and a spring in her step, as if she were bursting with confidence. She broke the remaining conventions of royal dress consistent with the dignity of the mother of the future king: in other words, she allowed herself to wear sunglasses, jeans, nail polish and short skirts.

She had moved out of Highgrove, making a bonfire of her possessions there, and taking with her the butler, Paul Burrell, whom she called 'my rock'. She had carried out faultlessly her first official overseas visit since the separation, to Nepal. In spite of these large steps to independence, she had never been more anxious about the future. On Christmas Day 1993 she reached a watershed when, after church with the royal family at Sandringham, she left her sons and was driven back to London to have lunch by herself at Kensington Palace. That the most famous woman on earth should have nobody to turn to on that day is a reminder of what she had lost in her thirteen-year saga with the royal family.

The next question was how Diana would cope on the evening when Prince Charles was to lay his soul bare on television, in an interview with Jonathan Dimbleby. She was scheduled to attend a gala dinner at the Serpentine Gallery in London's Hyde Park. The eyes of the world were on her.

The way to get the best from Diana was to challenge her. While the British public still loved her, the press was divided. The tabloids supported her, but as part of the establishment backlash, the broadsheets, and even some of the snobbier glossies, turned against her. She was still stinging from the bitchiest of attacks in a sophisticated young British society magazine, two months previously. *Tatler* had lambasted Diana's 'sympathy wardrobe' by labelling her an 'Essex girl': a snob denunciation of suburban English style that implied being overdressed during the day, and not afraid to display it. 'The Princess has dismissed her bodyguards, relinquished her public duties and... mislaid her style advisors,' wrote *Tatler*, before condemning items of her recent appearance as 'dead common'. They cited her 'frosted-tip hair-dos,' her 'mix 'n' mess co-ordinating two pieces', 'pastel-shade suits twinned with baby-pink pumps' and 'matching his 'n' hers leather blousons' worn by Diana and her private detective Ken Wharfe on an outing with William and Harry to Thorpe Park, a theme park near London. This editorial was unprecedented and painful, especially as *Tatler*'s sister magazine, *Vogue*, still had a hand in Diana's wardrobe and published annual eulogies on the Princess's elegance. Whatever Diana was about to wear for the gala dinner, the odds were that it would be dark and sophisticated.

"Diana"

When the evening arrived, Diana almost ran across the gravel from the limousine. As she unfolded from the car and strode forward vigorously on her high black silk heels and her long black silk legs, stretching out her arm to shake hands with Lord Palumbo, she was poetry in motion. Her short wheat-coloured hair caught the sun, her head was high, her dazzling smile was immense and her dress was fabulous: the briefest off-the-shoulder black chiffon with a scarf panel flying behind her from the waist. She wore her favourite pearl choker with the egg-sized sapphire, and her matching engagement ring. She was lightly tanned, and the nails of her strong hands were painted poppy red.

She could not have got her message across more clearly had she shouted it to the sky: 'I am not a victim any more!' The Americans christened it the 'I'll Show You' dress, and the 'Vengeance Dress'.

Besides her wedding dress, it was to be her most famous frock.

The *Telegraph Magazine* was to describe it as, 'The pièce de résistance... the brave, wicked, historic little "Serpentine Cocktail", possibly the most strategic dress ever worn by a woman in modern times. This was the devastating wisp of black chiffon with which Diana flipped her husband clean off the front pages the morning after his damaging televised interview. This is a dress that shows Diana, Princess of Wales fully in command of a sense of her own value.'

The Princess had chosen a dress by a relatively unknown designer, the Athens-trained Greek Christina Stambolian, who was now catapulted into the limelight. Diana had not intended to wear it. It wasn't even new. She had bought it eight months previously, on a fine October Saturday after lunching with her brother at her favourite restaurant, San Lorenzo. Emerging into Beauchamp Place in Mayfair, the sister and brother had walked into Stambolian's shop where the Earl helped her choose a red-and-black dress and a pleated blouse off the peg. Then Diana turned to the designer and said, 'I want a dress for a special occasion.' In fact, she had no occasion in mind. 'I told the Princess that she should wear black,' says Christina Stambolian, who had longed to dress Diana. As the measurements were taken, the designer sat down and did a quick drawing. Diana smiled at the drawing, but demurred. Wouldn't it be too bare? The designer responded briefly, 'Why not?' and Earl Spencer added his endorsement. A couple of fittings later, it was hanging in the walk-in wardrobe in Kensington Palace, where it remained unworn until the memorable evening.

Christina Stambolian loves to tell the story of the 'Vengeance Dress'. 'I was so thrilled to see Diana wear it on that night of all nights,' she says. 'She chose not to play the scene like Odette, innocent in white. She was clearly angry.

previous pages and opposite The notorious little black dress with which Diana pushed Charles off the front pages on the evening he gave his televized interview and admitted to adultery with Camilla Parker-Bowles. By Christina Stambolian, the dress had been hanging in Diana's cupboard unworn for eight months. Now it was suddenly her most famous dress. She wore it with the highest heels, the reddest nail polish and the biggest sapphire in London.

above and opposite Diana had never confined herself to British designers, but the perception was that she always wore British in public. Now the separation had freed her to wear Italian and French designers as and when she chose. Valentino made this above-the-knee burgundy velvet dress with scalloped and panelled bodice, and embroidered skirt. She wore it in Hong Kong and at the Barbican in 1992.

She played it like Odile, in black. She wore bright red nail enamel, which we had never seen her do before. She was saying, "Let's be wicked tonight!"' When she next met the Princess at the reception for the clothes auction at Christie's, the designer was able to tell Diana how proud she had made her. 'The Princess cupped her hand round my ear and whispered to me "I had a job to get into that little dress that night!"'

The story behind her choice is equally interesting, involving her faithful butler, Paul Burrell. Now that William and Harry had departed for boarding school, it was often Burrell whom Diana asked, 'How do I look? What do you think – this dress or that one?' As usual, the Princess had planned what to wear ahead of time. The story goes that the designer of the dress she had planned to wear had taken the opportunity to tell the press ahead of time of her intention. Diana, always on her guard against being exploited for publicity, was annoyed and looked for another dress to wear.

She chose an alternative and, as usual, pressed the bell to
call her style-conscious butler for his opinion. He vetoed the
dress at once. He reminded her that this was a very special night,
that she needed the most feminine and beautiful dress of all –
something to make her feel proud and confident. He felt it had
to be black, a dress that would command a lot of attention and
send a strong message. Together, they went through the clothes
hanging in her walk-in wardrobe, and it was Paul Burrell who pulled
out the unworn Stambolian chiffon dress and said that this was the
one. With his usual brotherly encouragement, Burrell reminded his boss
to walk confidently from the car, keeping her head up, and to give Lord
Palumbo the kind of handshake that meant business. The performance
worked brilliantly. The public adored it: Diana was back and adding
to the gaiety of the nation.

above The dress was
sophisticated and black, but
it was low-cut and backless.
In matt velvet with glossy bead
edging, Diana wore it for her
first foreign engagement after
her 'withdrawal' from public
life to a charity function in
Versailles, France in 1994.

Since the separation and her removal from conventional royal life, she had
become very clear about what she wanted her public image to be. Dressing
down or dressing up, she dressed for political reasons. She had arrived at a
hallmark, feminine look that worked for her, and she was no longer very
interested in experimenting. From a narrower field, she would hunt down the
dress that did the job wherever it came from. It had been recognized for some
time, even before the separation, that Diana's clothes were no longer entirely
British. While there had been a minor fuss about her choice of a non-British
car, and she now leased a £14,000-a-year Jaguar, it was harder for the press
to know where she did her fashion shopping.

In fact, she had always bought clothes for her private life from the famous
Italian, French and American designer shops. An indication of how many buys
she made may be the estimated £12,000 she spent at Chanel in one year. In
public she appeared in Chanel coats and suits, 'cocktail' suits and dresses by
Valentino or John Galliano, and had been frequently seen in Ralph Lauren
on the polo field. She also bought from Yves Saint Laurent, Moschino, Escada,
Louis Feraud, MaxMara and Mondi. The rock 'n' roll couturier Versace was
beginning to shower her with clothes, as Valentino always had. 'I am quite
used to assessing the taste,' explains Valentino. 'I knew what she would love
and what she wouldn't like. I had her measurements, of course, and when I
thought of something that was good and right for her, I would send sketches
and colours, both for official events and for her privately. Then I would send
the dress, with shoes and bag to match.' Quite possibly these unsolicited clothes
from foreign designers were sent as gifts: certainly the designers loved her to
wear their clothes, and perhaps as a 'half royal' the Princess did not feel obliged
to be so punctilious as formerly.

One of her favourite British designers was the quiet, self-effacing Jacques Azagury whom she had met in 1985 on his stall at the London Designer Collections. She had introduced herself with a dazzling smile and a statement of the obvious: 'I am the Princess of Wales!' 'I know!' responded the designer with an equally wide grin. He noticed that she glanced several times at a dress that she was to buy from him three weeks later. With blue stars embroidered on a black bodice, and a skirt in brilliant blue organza tied with a bow, it was one of the most photographed dresses she wore on trips to Florence and Toronto. Since then, he had been one of her favourite designers, producing many of her sexiest and simplest evening dresses and always urging her to shorten her hems even more. In the 1990s, when Diana had found her fashion form she was a regular customer. As she told him, 'I know what I am going to find, and I know I'll like

left By 1993 Diana preferred a slimmer look. This narrow Victor Edelstein dress in blue silk crepe was high cut in the front, and crossed over at the back.

it. That's why I don't ask for anything special.' It was from Azagury that she bought the red dress that she wore to the Red Cross Ball in 1997 – proving that she was still sending the liveliest and simplest of messages through what she wore.

Diana, during this period, made only two fashion mistakes that anyone remembers. Both were extreme looks and worn to fashion events in New York. There was the Dior dress that made her look exactly as if she was wearing a night-dress, and the hairstyle that looked as if she had just got out of the shower. Sam McKnight, the hairdresser who had given Diana her successful, modern crop, and regularly flew across the Atlantic to cut her hair, persuaded her to accompany the Walker blue silk dress she wore to the CFDA awards in New York with a radical 'wet look' such as the supermodels were wearing at the time. It was reminiscent of the photographs of her wonderful appearance at the open air Pavarotti concert in Hyde Park, when she was drenched in rain, naturally dishevelled and laughing: but somehow it went wrong. Those were the last two times that Diana ever succumbed to becoming a fashion victim.

A directional new London designer, Amanda Wakeley, caught Diana's eye the moment she set up shop on her own in 1992. Wakeley makes subtle, luxurious clothes that accorded with Diana's settled attitude to what she would wear. 'Our not making trend statements may have appealed to her,' says the beautiful blonde designer today. 'Her look was becoming cleaner and simpler

opposite and right Diana loved off-the-shoulder and halterneck dresses in the early nineties, because they showed off her spectacular gym-toned shoulders. She wore this Catherine Walker dress of pistachio and cream silk crepe, buttoned with paste and slit to the knee to a premiere of *Accidental Hero* in 1993. The fashion press commented that she had now overdeveloped her shoulders and Walker should have been covering them up.

all the time, but she always thought she needed to do the "bells and whistles" for the public, because they expected the glamour, the colour and the hats.

'She bought suits and many weekend clothes such as cashmeres and suede pants. She bought clothes that were never seen in public, like the navy crêpe trouser suit with a big pearl tassel.'

If Diana liked the clothes because they didn't grab attention, she also found they gave her confidence. The blackberry-coloured wool suit with the velvet trim that she wore to give the Birthright speech was Amanda Wakeley's, as was the bottle-green suit she wore for her 'resignation' speech. 'Diana would stroke garments. She loved the feel of suede and cashmere, and I was delighted one day when I ran into her leaving the gym at the Harbour Club in my big cashmere sweater with turnback silk cuffs.'

Amanda Wakeley's influence helped lead Diana to the idea of departing from the 'big fashion numbers' in due course. But how could she abandon the glamour when it was her lifeline to popularity? She was the only member of the royal family who needed the public as much as the public needed her, and her very lack of a defined role increased the adulation of the masses. As Simone de Beauvoir said of Greta Garbo, 'She had a kind of emptiness into which anything could be projected.'

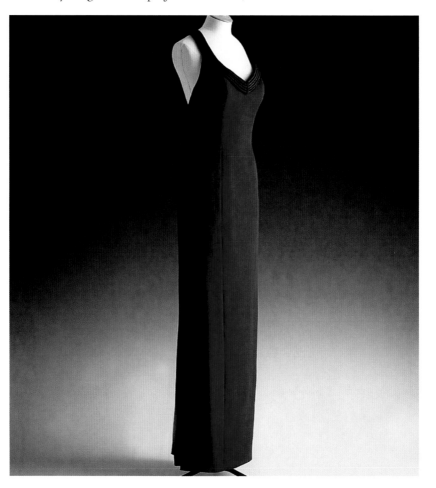

above and right The 'wet look' hair that Diana wore to present the CFDA awards in New York in 1996 was one of her last fashion mistakes. The idea was to reproduce the way she had looked when she had been drenched with rain at Luciano Pavarotti's open-air concert in 1991: tousled, laughing and ravishing. Unfortunately the hair went wrong, and it was said that she looked as if she had just stepped out of the shower. Diana wore her favourite sapphire and pearl choker with a Catherine Walker dress of blue satin. The edging was made of five satin rouleaux which separated at the shoulders and crossed over the back.

opposite New York and fashion events seemed to shake Diana's fashion poise – perhaps because she was trying too hard. At a Costume Institute gala at the Metropolitan Museum in 1996, she wore a navy dress by John Galliano for Dior that looked as if she was wearing her petticoat. It was the first dress by Galliano, the couturier for the eminent Paris fashion house, and Diana wanted to support the talented designer. At the fitting at Kensington Palace, Diana had suggested some alterations to the design, and the fact that she wore the satin coat over the dress suggests that she had reservations. The exercise finally convinced Diana that avant garde fashion was not for princesses.

There was not a newspaper or magazine in the land which didn't appreciate her ability to manipulate the public perception of her through the images she chose to show. At the end of 1995, the *Daily Mail* hailed her as the 'undisputed Queen of haute couture', and *Hello!* magazine subjected 35 photographs of Diana's outfits throughout the year to selection by a dozen international couturiers. Included were clothes by Versace, Jasper Conran, Jacques Azagury, Tomasz Starzewski, Edina Ronay, John Galliano and Roland Klein. The winner was a Catherine Walker tailored black crêpe which, 'underlined her status as wronged wife, cut as it was in the style favoured by the most stylish example of that ilk, Jackie O.'

In the era of the supermodel, Diana was fascinated by beautiful images of women. On one occasion, she had asked photographer Patrick Demarchelier to bring Linda Evangelista, the most famous model of her day, to meet her. For inspiration towards finding her own identity in fashion, however, the

left In 1997, and still sending signals through her clothes, Diana ordered Christian Dior's Prince-of-Wales check suit with the trousers and the skirt. The frayed-edge lapels were much copied by middle-range manufacturers.

left In 1995 it was clear that Diana was beginning to enjoy her new independent life. She wore this Christian Lacroix short red showpiece dress at the Petit Palais in Paris. With its bodice tied with a bow, and lipstick, nail polish and high red heels to match, she showed off her well-exercised figure and rejoiced in looking anything but royal.

Princess was more interested in movie stars: constantly photographed beauties whose personalities were more important than their clothes. 'Very Audrey Hepburn!' she might comment when Philip Somerville offered her a flowerpot hat similar to the ones the star used to wear with her barrel-cut Givenchy coats. In Diana's first floor sitting room at Kensington Palace she kept on display a series of framed, privately taken photographs of her imitating Audrey Hepburn in outfits from the movie *Breakfast at Tiffany's*. Once in a while she would try on a dress that she knew was too revealing for her, and camp it up for the designer, putting her hands on her hips and walking like Marilyn Monroe in *Some Like it Hot*.

right Diana's hallmark 'function'
uniform in the year of her
Panorama interview was a big
flattering hat and crisp suit in
a pastel colour, with special
buttons and – as often as not
– fake jewellery from Theo
Fennell or Butler & Wilson.
She is pictured here at the
VE day celebrations in 1995.

opposite In a devastatingly chic
hat and suit that emphasized her
summer suntan, Diana stole all
the limelight at the VJ Parade in
1995, when she had to sit on
the red carpet alongside Prince
Charles. She was already
planning her *Panorama*
television broadcast, and
would soon be fighting to
keep her royal title. Meanwhile
Diana and Charles put the boys
between them and looked in
opposite directions. Her hat
of white synamay straw with
its navy satin band was by
Philip Somerville, and
complemented the Tomasz
Starzewski suit beautifully.

But if there was one world star who Diana really did compare herself with,
study and copy, it was Jackie Kennedy. The wife of the American president,
later the wife of the Greek ship owner Aristotle Onassis, had a significance
for Diana that came of many similarities. Jackie had been as stylish, charismatic,
admired and emulated as Diana, and her life was as full, as Diana's was and
would become, of world-shaking crises and astonishing, even horrifying
developments. Like Diana, she was supposed to be the luckiest woman in the
world, travelling the globe in an official capacity, and captivating world leaders.
Both Jack Kennedy and Prince Charles had joked, on state visits, that they
were merely there to accompany their famous wives. Like Diana, Jackie's real
world centred on her children and she was terrified of losing her children to
the family she had married into. Like Diana, she had spent fortunes on her
clothes and was given fabulous jewels. Like Diana, Jackie Kennedy has been
called the greatest single influence in modern fashion history.

right This Versace sketch was of the metallic blue dress studded and beaded in gold that Diana wore to be photographed by Patrick Demarchelier. The dress fitted like a glove and the photographer encouraged her to cut her hair shorter and tone down her make-up. After the sitting it was clear that she had modernized her look, and with it her outlook.

message in itself. It is an afterthought... a non-hat. The focus should be on the face.'

When Jackie wore the hat at the inaugural with her fawn coat, it was suddenly as if the world knew of no other kind of headgear. My design, which would become known as the pillbox hat, became a national trend.'

'Diana adored pillboxes,' confirms Philip Somerville. 'And she liked to wear them as Jackie Kennedy did, on the back of the head, to show her thick fringe. Sometimes I wanted her to wear it another way, and I would push her hair out of the way. She always said, "O, Mr Somerville, can't I have my fringe back?"'

'Once she asked me, "Do you think, one day, people will think of me as the Jackie Kennedy of my day?"' On her Washington visit, Diana was hailed as precisely that – the new Jackie Kennedy, more royal than the royals.

If only the fleeting memory of Diana in the courageous Stambolian

opposite By the time she attended this gala evening at the ballet, one of her first public engagements since agreeing to the divorce, Diana had arrived at the perfect formula for minimal chic. She wore an simple cream sheath dress by Catherine Walker, with gold embroidery. The strappy high-heeled shoes were by Jimmy Choo; she had several pairs in different colours.

above and opposite The deep neckline of this showstopping red lace cocktail dress was apparently only held in place by a loop of satin ribbon. It was made by Catherine Walker for Diana's visit to Argentina in 1995. The Princess was flaunting her legs in shorter and shorter skirts, and the exuberance of the solitary royal inspired 'bravos' from the citizens of Buenos Aires.

dress could have been left as her overriding image of the early nineties. But only a couple of months later an embarrassing story came to light that Diana had been making 'nuisance calls' to a millionaire art dealer, ringing him continually and putting the phone down when his wife answered. She held secret meetings with *Daily Mail* journalist Richard Kay and, damningly, only half denied the accusations. Once again the press raised questions about her state of mind. The *Observer* asked, 'Has Diana finally flipped? One hesitates to ask it, but is she bonkers?... There has been speculation that she could be approaching some kind of breakdown.' She had voluntarily given up her protection officers, and now was seen running from photographers, and shouting at them in the street. Seen in tears, she was quickly nicknamed 'The Princess of Wails'.

She also agonized over the addition of a pretty and charming young woman, Tiggy Legge-Bourke, to act as surrogate mother to the boys in the holidays they spent with Charles. Diana saw less of her beloved sons than ever, and the idea of another woman putting them to bed and taking them on picnics was a source of great pain.

Neither truly married nor truly single, deprived of normal loving relationships, the Princess's attempts to reach out to men had always ended in merciless scrutiny or betrayal. As a modern, separated woman, there was no reason why Diana should not have affairs, and it would have made a perfect scenario had she now fallen into the arms of an attractive unattached jet-setting billionaire. Even if she ever met such a man, the press would make it extremely difficult for the relationship to move into a one-to-one affair. She admired Imran Khan, who married Jemima Goldsmith, daughter of one of Diana's 'mother' mentors, and she may have been trying to find a comparable figure.

Meanwhile, Diana's press relations oscillated between adulation and recrimination. At Versailles in 1995, in contrast to her previous all-white evening appearances in Paris, she wore black. Catherine Walker had made her a backless halterneck column with a fluid wrapped skirt and edged with beading. The result was a brilliantly smiling Diana who, 'dazzled, glittered, radiated, stunned and shone'. Shortly afterwards, her friendship with Will Carling, former England rugby captain, came under scrutiny. Now even the *Sun*, who had always backed the Princess, ran headlines such as, 'Two-faced Diana'.

It didn't help her that she had so publicly cut down on her charity work. In fact, she had only pruned the number of patronages and handshaking events, and continued her close encounters with the needy and the sick. Had she been an ordinary woman with an ordinary career, her years of exceptional work would by now have qualified her for promotion. She granted this to herself by accepting a job as an international federation representative with the Red Cross Advisory Commission. She was not, however, cut out for executive work. She much preferred the private, low-key work she undertook for her remaining cherished causes, and went to meet people in homes and hospices as many as four times a week.

'As long as the Princess's great beauty was shown compassionately, tending the sick and needy, it was beauty matched with goodness,' commented the *Sunday Telegraph*. 'But when she retired from... charity work, no one predicted how trivial and self-indulgent her private life would appear to be. Now our innocent nursery school assistant is turned into a café society jet-setter, addicted to the telephone and trying to escape the photographers' lens by using the back door of an exclusive London health club synonymous with a life of leisure.'

below Chicago fell to Diana's glamour and charm on her three-day visit there in June 1996. After a day spent at Cook County Hospital, meeting victims of gunshot wounds and knifings, she changed into this violet Versace dress for a fundraising banquet. She flew out saying, 'I love Chicago'.

opposite Diana's simple Versace dresses were becoming her trademark as early as 1995, when she wore this cream shift to a Pavarotti concert for the children of Bosnia in Italy.

right Just before Charles' own low-key visit to America, Diana slipped into Washington DC, and won all hearts: the press announced it as one of Diana's brilliant 'spoilers'. Still sending signals, Diana wore a red dress by Jacques Azagury for the Washington international fundraising dinner for the Red Cross. The high bodice was embroidered with bugle beads.

Confronted once again by a bad press, Diana dreaded to lose the public support she had won, against all odds, with the publication of the book. She had made her voice heard, and found it empowering. She determined that the next time she would speak directly to the people in a television interview. She had agreed to give a long and personal interview to journalist Martin Bashir for the BBC's flagship current affairs programme, *Panorama*. The operation was conducted in complete secrecy. Diana dismissed her staff for the day, and the crew arrived at Kensington Palace on a Sunday, with compact cameras that would not attract attention. Even the governors of the BBC were kept in the dark.

right Diana upstages Imran Khan in April 1996, wearing the *shalwar kameez* on her visit to Pakistan. She was criticized for appearing to support a man involved in a political campaign, but Diana maintained she had come to meet her friends, Imran and wife Jemima – and to see his cancer hospital.

The interview was a sensation. The largest audience of any television documentary in broadcasting history sat back to watch Diana discuss her husband, her children, her life and her hopes for the future. Several phrases will go down in history, never to be forgotten, notably 'There were three of us in this marriage so it was a bit crowded,' and, 'I would like to be a Queen in people's hearts.' She even cast doubts over Prince Charles's future as king. Just four weeks later, the Queen wrote personally to both the Prince and Princess requesting that they get the divorce over with as soon as possible.

On Wednesday, 28 February 1996, a date the Princess described as the saddest day of her life, she signed her agreement to an uncontested divorce. The new independent Diana made a decision to announce the news to the world in her own words, so that she could give precedence to the terms she considered most important.

'The Princess of Wales has agreed to Prince Charles's request for a divorce. The Princess will continue to be involved in all decisions relating to the children and will remain at Kensington Palace, with offices in St James's Palace.

above and opposite Diana wore Jacques Azagury's black dress with an embroidered sequin bodice to receive a humanitarian award from Henry Kissinger in New York in 1995: on her left are Colin Powell and Barbara Walters. Diana also wore this dress out in London on the evening her *Panorama* interview was broadcast. Two weeks before she died, she sent Azagury a framed and mounted trio of photographs of herself in his last three dresses, including this one.

December '95
lace & georgette
evening dress
for:
Diana: Princess
of Wales.

179

opposite Diana wore this simple pale-pink Catherine Walker suit with Versace's 'Lady Di' handbag for an Awards lunch at the Savoy in London in March 1997. No longer 'Her Royal Highness', her public pulling power refused to dissipate: she was still the focus of attention wherever she went.

The Princess of Wales will retain the title and be known as Diana, Princess of Wales.'

She had finally gone too far. The Queen authorized an icy public rebuke to her daughter-in-law, in which she warned that details concerning the settlement, future role and title remained to be settled. Five months of negotiations later, when the marriage came to an end with the decree absolute on 28 August 1996, it was clear how Diana was to be punished. The Princess was given offices at St James's Palace and a payment estimated at £17 million. But she lost her title. She was no longer 'Her Royal Highness'.

above In February 1997, Diana attended the film premiere of *In Love and War* wearing a tight-fitting blue embroidered dress by Catherine Walker.

Icon

T he Diana who could be seen walking alone along the pavements of Knightsbridge in the months preceding her death wore sunglasses and fake pearls, a sleeveless shift by Versace that fitted like a glove, bare legs and flat beige pumps by Jimmy Choo. Just as she emerged during the eighties like a butterfly from a chrysalis, she now passed into a personal style beyond the vicissitudes of fashion.

'In the last few years', wrote Sarah Mower in *The Times Magazine*, in September 1997, 'Diana had reached her ultimate state of grace. Here was a woman so in control of the clothes she wore, the accessories she chose, the casual raked-back way that she did her hair, that she had performed the highest feat of chic for herself: what she was wearing had ceased to matter. All you saw was her and all you noticed was that she looked fantastic.'

She had come full circle since members of the royal household watched her scanning her press coverage as though searching for clues to her own identity. She did not dress for sympathy any more, but in a uniform of flattering, comfortable dresses that emphasized, without revealing, her figure. In all probability, she didn't even bother to read the dictums of the newspaper fashion police, who now declared that her shoulders were too heavy for low-cut, sleeveless dresses, due to the many hours she had spent in the gym. The famous fashion epigram 'less is more' defined her new brand of elegance.

right This short navy dress with a flared skirt made for Diana's private wardrobe, was designed by Roland Klein, who dressed her throughout her life. She asked him to shorten the skirt; then to shorten it again. It was the last dress he made for her.

'The new Diana looked really great,' says Amanda Wakeley. 'Clean lines, simple shapes, luxurious fabrics – that's where she was coming from. She no longer felt she had to do the fashion number for the public with glamour, colour and hats. The way she looked that final year came from feeling good about herself at last.'

Diana had transformed herself yet again, saying, 'From now on, I am going to own myself and be true to myself. I no longer want to live someone else's idea of what and who I should be.' She never wore a hat. Her hair was straight, short and blew about naturally, looking a little messy. She gave up ringing her eyes with blue khol, but in Paris, for the first time in her life, she was seen wearing scarlet lipstick. There was a fraction more curve to her figure. She had virtually given up wearing jewellery. As Valentino says, 'She became increasingly simple in the way she dressed. I remember meeting her on one occasion when she was wearing pearl earrings. I was amused to see they were fake, because I had spotted them in a glass case in the Metropolitan Museum!'

The late Gianni Versace was the key designer for Diana in her last years, helping her to achieve what fashion people call 'minimal chic'. When he called at Kensington Palace with a selection of new suits and dresses for spring, shortly before his own death, he found her more serene than he had ever known her. 'She has found herself,' he said, 'and the way she wants to live.'

His sister, Donatella, who now heads up the famous Italian fashion house, explains that Diana used to visit the Versace boutique like a normal customer, buying jeans, sunglasses or handbags each time. Versace designed a special handbag for her, and customers would ask for the 'Lady D'. The Princess could order the clothes directly from sketches or videos because they had several toiles made for her in different fabrics, carefully fitted so that her exact size was always available. They could then make up whatever the Princess ordered, and their premier, Signora Biagini, always attended the fittings either at the boutique or Kensington Palace.

previous page It is fascinating to compare Diana here, in 1997 with the picture taken before her engagement on page 24. Same woman, same street, but worlds apart in terms of experience and style. This was the effortless 'minimal chic' which all her designers, past and present, recognized and applauded in the last few years of her life.

opposite Formal or casual, Diana got it right. Her 'trademark' looks, from one-shoulder dresses to jewelled headbands, must include the way she dressed a thousand times for her regular workouts at the Chelsea Harbour Club.

'In 1995, my bother dedicated a collection to the Princess, calling it "Conservative Chic"', Donatella remembers. 'The look was epitomized by the slim knee-length shift dress in a pastel colour that the Princess liked to wear as she changed into a modern, independent and stylish woman. Those dresses emphasized her silhouette and her slim figure. She was a woman who moved with the times and understood what suited her'.

Diana had wondered whether, in the future, she would be remembered as the Marilyn Monroe or Jackie Kennedy of her day, as she achieved iconic status, her fame and mystique equalled theirs. Her intensive sixteen-year course in fashion had left her with the clearest idea of what worked for her. She became, for the first time in her life, a speedy shopper. As one designer remembers it, she could pick two or three outfits and be out of his shop in 20 minutes. Like other style icons the industry had vied to dress, women such as Diana Vreeland, Lady Diana Cooper, Lauren Bacall, Grace Kelly and Audrey Hepburn, Diana had transcended fashion. Instead of showing her every sample, the designers worked the Diana 'look' into their collections. It is not too much to say that the current extreme simplification in fashion, with its jacket-based 'capsule wardrobes' including a plain shift dress and high heels have influenced us all.

As Bruce Oldfield says, 'Diana began by going off into fashion like a loose cannon, needing a stylist. In the last years of her life, she managed that look of greyhound sleekness as if she had dashed in, slipped on a dress, combed her hair and run out again. In the end, it was all about her presence. She exuded this magnetic force. She didn't have to do much, but she was always the centre of any room.'

The pundits who had predicted that the 'electric charge' between the Princess and the public would dissipate on her separation from the Prince, were proved quite wrong. Indeed, by losing her royal title, and as a loving mother in danger of losing her influence over her sons' lives, Diana could be seen as a martyr. She was protected from her detractors by the strength of public affection and sympathy, an emotional bond which would all too soon make itself unforgettably felt. In a sense, even the combined forces of the House of Lords, the Church of England, academe and royalists, could not now denigrate Diana.

All her life she had had a pathological reluctance to take any part of the blame, but now she had finally taken responsibility for her own actions by admitting to an adulterous affair of her own, and for not seeming whiter than white. The sense of betrayal that the public felt when they discovered that few among the royal family had been able to meet the standards of family life that they had held up for the public to follow, inclined them not to judge her too

above For the New York party, Diana wore the same shift, but this time embroidered with coffee-coloured roses in crystals and sequins, with her Jimmy Choo three-inch heels. New York had brought out the fashion victim in Diana on two previous occasions. Now New Yorkers saw a new Diana, who knew what suited her and was going to stick to it.

opposite At the previews of the Christie's sale of her evening dresses, Diana thanked Catherine Walker by wearing two of her embroidered shift dresses. To the London party she wore a short, revealing sheath of pale blue embroidered in blue and silver. With her blonde hair and suntan, Diana looked happy and triumphant.

harshly. As a result of the succession of unsavoury royal revelations, and from recognition of Diana's affiliation with the charity ethos, there was a new non-judgemental mood in the country. Her message now was, 'I am not perfect, but I am your Queen of Hearts.' She continued to get a bad press in the last few months of her life, but she was now a national obsession and so deeply rooted in the British psyche that newspaper criticism only demonstrated as she had felt for some time, how far the press had lost touch with the mood of the mass public.

Losing the title of 'Her Royal Highness' in 1996 – although against her wishes – liberated her from 'function' dressing and gave her permission to be herself. It was a further and final step in the discarding of the old life. She had already let go of most of her servants, her ladies-in-waiting and her bodyguards. To signal this latest transformation and make her metamorphosis plain to the whole world, she now jettisoned the working wardrobe that had turned her into 'the jewel in the crown' between 1981 and 1996, and closed that part of her life forever.

Roland Klein remembers an occasion from that last year of her life when he was about to show Diana some evening dresses. She shook her head and told him, 'I do not wear evening dresses anymore – I have nowhere to go!' 'I laughed of course', he says, 'but later on I began to think she meant it.'

The idea for the Christie's auction was Prince William's, as Diana testified on the first page of the lush catalogue, her handwriting flowing over her new cream writing paper under the coronated crimson initial 'D'. It was not just a public farewell to the most sumptuous working wardrobe in the world, it was also a resounding response to all those press complaints over the years about the money she had spent on frocks. The 79 dresses – lot thirteen was deleted for superstitious reasons – took place in New York in June 1997, with the proceeds benefiting AIDS and cancer charities.

The sale was cannily handled by Meredith Etherington-Smith, Christie's creative director, in great secrecy. Diana chose Snowdon to take half a dozen photographs for the catalogue, putting on the chosen dresses for the last time. She wore several more for the fashion photographer, Mario Testino. These photographs, which showed Diana more relaxed than any other photographer had caught her before, appeared in the magazine *Vanity Fair* just before the sale.

The dresses had, as Christie's chairman Christopher Balfour said, 'a sort of magic about them'. They had a global familiarity, for everyone had seen them in photographs. They were each, in Etherington-Smith's words, 'mini-biographies'. To see them for real conferred on them Diana's own mystique and reminded the world of each royal milestone. As the *Daily Mail* put it, they were 'The Ups and Gowns of Diana's Life'.

below In New York for the auction, Diana walked the streets of Manhattan in a peppermint green suit by Chanel.

First, the dresses were put on display in London, where four thousand people filed through the auction rooms to view them over four days. At the London party, Diana, her hair a little blonded, wore a Catherine Walker shift embroidered in pale blue and silver, an aquamarine ring and small drop earrings. Then under tight security, the dresses were flown to New York and arranged in Christie's Park Avenue exhibition halls. There, around five thousand more people came to see the dresses for themselves and millions more saw them through the almost constant television coverage. The crowds camping out in the boiling summer heat to see Diana, took up their positions six hours before the Princess's arrival for this party, where she wore another Walker shift, this time embroidered in pale coffee-coloured roses in sequins and crystals.

The auction on the 25 June raised $3,258,750 from the dresses and the sale of the catalogues, and made Diana, at a stroke, one of the world's great philanthropists. The highest price of $222,500 was for the blue velvet Victor

above Lot 19, a Catherine Walker dress and bolero made for the Indian tour of 1992, goes under the hammer. Diana would never wear dresses like this again.

opposite For a visit to a Hindu temple in Neasden, London in the year of her death – one of her last public engagements – Diana revived the look of the working princess, wearing a Catherine Walker dress with sleeves and calf-length skirt.

Edelstein dress that Diana had worn to dance with John Travolta at the White House; the 'Elvis' dress and jacket with the stand-up collar embroidered with pearls and sequins, went for $151,000 and Diana's own favourite, the Victor Edelstein dress with Hurel embroidery, worn to a state banquet at the Elysée Palace, went for $203,750. It was a triumph and every triumph now gave her lasting happiness, because any success was hers and hers alone. It is possible that she intended to have a further clothes auction, for she now wrote to several girlfriends and asked if they would return clothes that she had passed on to them.

She proved in the last year of her life, as her brother was to say in his funeral tribute, that she needed no royal title to continue to generate her particular brand of magic. What had a title or clothes to do with 'Gods work on earth'? The personal value of Diana's work was expressed by the mother of a severely

above A month before her death, Diana's last public engagement was to visit a children's centre on the outskirts of London. When not visiting a place of worship, Diana wore what suited her best – the little shift dress. It had taken sixteen years for her to dress the same in public as she did in private.

191

brain-damaged young man with whom she spent time at a Barnardo's centre for disadvantaged and handicapped children. Diana knelt on the floor beside the sofa where he was propped up between his parents, put her face close to his and spoke to him for several minutes so quietly that only he could hear. His mother told reporters afterwards, 'I feel if my kid is acceptable to Diana, then he is acceptable to everybody.'

In assuaging her lifelong feelings of unworthiness, the 'Work' had given her more happiness than anything else, other than her two boys. One of her most rewarding moments came in December 1996 when she was presented by Dr Henry Kissinger with the Humanitarian of the Year Award at a ceremony in New York. Paying hommage to her 'luminous personality' he praised the way she had 'aligned herself with the ill, the suffering and the downtrodden.'

below Because of her tireless work for the campaign against landmines in Angola, Diana is probably best remembered as she is pictured here – in Armani jeans and a plain cotton shirt.

She had said in her television interview that she wanted to be an ambassador for the country: 'I have got tremendous knowledge about people and how to communicate, and I want to use it.' She had been denied that role, but through her support of various charities, she saw another way to do what she had always wanted and give her life a proper and serious purpose. Tony Blair was supportive of her wish for a role, and invited her to meet him on a couple of occasions to discuss ways of achieving it. She now went straight to the heart of the landmines issue and was able, in the Prime Minister's words, 'to clarify for the people what was the right thing to do.'

'I wanted to do more than just read about statistics,' she said, 'my purpose was simple – to heighten global awareness of the human suffering caused by these evil weapons.'

She had decided to accompany Red Cross officials and a BBC film crew to publicize their work in Angola. Doubts were cast on the wisdom of her involvement in such a politically sensitive subject and there were objections to her attending a meeting of the all-party landmines eradication group in the House of Commons. This did not stop her from going. And so, in January 1997, a khaki clad Diana trekked through bleak Angola, consoling victims of anti-personnel mines and walking through a minefield for the benefit of the world's press photographers. The abiding memory

right For Diana's rare public appearances, she simply wore long versions of her daytime shifts. This glittering black low-cut dress with tailored bows on the satin shoulder straps was given to Diana as a thirty-sixth birthday present by Jacques Azagury. She wore it on her birthday to a gala dinner at the Tate Gallery in London.

of Diana's clothes in that last year was of her in the most ordinary of sleeveless cotton shirts and pants on this trip. The distinguished *Daily Telegraph* columnist Bill Deedes admitted that he had doubted the value of her visit until he saw her in action. 'I formed the impression that if she is given the right mission she almost moves out of herself and becomes a different person altogether. You might say of her that she is looking for a serious role. She remains, in my mind, extremely important because she has a very big influence in the life of Prince William, about whom she thinks a great deal, of whom she's very proud, and of whom she wants to make something very worthwhile. I think compassion is what she's trying to bring to her son's life.'

But, even as Diana flew into Bosnia on her last mission, she was telephoning the latest man in her life, Dodi Fayed. A playboy with a reputed $100,000 a month income, he was the only son of Mohamed al-Fayed, the Egyptian multi-millionaire and owner of London's Harrods store, and his first wife, the late Samira Khashoggi. Diana stayed at the al-Fayed villa in St Tropez, in the south of France, with William and Harry, and went back for a cruise on the family yacht, *Jonikal*. She was, she told a friend, 'happier than I have ever been in my life – it's bliss.' When she told a batch of photographers 'you'll be surprised when you see what I do next,' many newspapers assumed that she would soon be married for the second time.

left Days from her death, Diana
allowed photographers
to photograph her on *Jonikal*,
the Al Fayed yacht, where
she was enjoying a holiday with
the new man in her life, Dodi
Fayed. This image of the solitary
Diana carries an emotional
charge that goes beyond the
message, 'I am free at last'.

above Diana had great
spiritual depths, but also
knew how to get this aspect
of herself across to the public
through the camera lens. This
picture of Diana, dressed to
meet the Pope at the Vatican
in 1985 in a full-length black
lace Catherine Walker dress,
when she was still intended
for Queen, speaks volumes in
terms of her dutiful nature and
aptitude for symbolic image.

Some acquaintances of Diana's evidently do not think that she meant that at all. It is their opinion that, buoyed by the success of her landmines campaign and the accompanying documentary, she had determined to follow that route to make a life for herself as a purposeful international journalist, airing chosen issues directly to the public through the medium of television. They say she was so serious about this that she planned to become a student to learn how to present television documentaries professionally. She was coming back from that last holiday in Paris with Dodi Fayed, for that final transformation. In the sixteen years during which Diana held the world's attention, she had never failed to surprise. We never knew what she would do next, and now we shall never know what she would have done next. Whatever she had wanted in the short term, all her life Diana entertained the same ambitions. She wanted to be useful in doing good and she wanted to be a modern woman. Ultimately she succeeded in both.

The news came through on radio and television bulletins early in the morning of Sunday 31 August 1997. During the night Prince William continually woke and felt something was wrong. The world woke up to the news that she was dead, and continued for most of the next day to find the news unbelievable. Gradually, as every branch of the media gave itself over to confirming and elaborating on what had happened, the shock set in.

It was, evidently, Paul Burrell the butler who was left to prepare Diana's body for the arrival of the Prince of Wales and Diana's two sisters, and it was Paul Burrell who requested from Catherine Walker the simple, black cocktail dress in which the Princess was ultimately buried, in a secret spot on the wooded island close to the family house.

Diana's name has appeared in headlines at least as many times in the six months since her death as in the six months before. It is as if we cannot let her go. She occupied our attention for so long that her going has left behind a void and sense of disorientation. In the extraordinary and unprecedented outpouring of grief witnessed around the world, but particularly in London, it finally came home to us that we had always underestimated her. With no qualifications for the job other than her ambition to be 'Queen of Hearts', the truth is that the winsome looks of the shy kindergarten teacher had concealed a personality who has changed the monarchy, softened the mood of the country, and even influenced in some small way the political priorities of the world.

No longer would the world respond to her beauty or her great talent for communication, her dedication to the people on the perimeter of society, or her emotional ability to unify the nation. Each one of the designers who helped to increase the powerful vocabulary of her fashion declared their sense of loss. I particularly remember Valentino's heart-broken 'she is never going to happen again in the world', Manolo Blahnik's 'she is one reason I stayed in England', Yuki's 'When she died, the days grew darker', and Jimmy Choo's 'She is top model to my heart'.

For the rest of us, there was the sense of great promise wasted. She would have made a perfect Queen, but she was gone – 'the unique, the complex, the extraordinary and irreplaceable Diana whose beauty, both internal and external, will never be extinguished from our minds.'

below This popular photograph, with its saintly overtones, shows Diana in a Catherine Walker dress and veil, worn during a visit to Egypt. Taken the year before Diana flew to visit Mother Teresa, who told her, 'You are doing God's work on Earth', the picture seems to prefigure Diana's transition to icon status.

Lots in Christie's Sale

D iana's wardrobe of state came under the hammer at Christie's, New York, on 25 June 1997.

It was the most celebrated auction since the Duchess of Windsor's jewels had fetched up to fifty times their estimated price, and excitement was at fever pitch. The fans outside in the summer heat on Manhattan's Park Avenue were offering the bidders up to $270 for their tickets. Inside the sale rooms, 1100 buyers were supplied with purple paddles to signal their bids.

The first dress by Gina Fratini doubled its opening price before most people had opened their catalogues, and climbed to a sale price of $85,000. Lot two, the infamous black dress Diana had worn the night Charles confessed to adultery in a television interview, was bought by Graeme and Briege MacKenzie, who run several Body Shop stores. An interior designer from Michigan, Ellen Petho, spent around $100,000 on four dresses, and an American television executive bought Diana's favourite, the satin dress and bolero by Victor Edelstein, as well as two Catherine Walker dresses. Maureen Rorech bought eleven dresses in the auction and five more from the winning bidders afterwards. A black velvet dress by Bruce Oldfield was sold for $36,800 at Christie's, and for $330,000 subsequently. Having taken the dresses around America, Maureen Rorech is now taking the dresses around the world. They will end their tour in London's Millennium Dome.

The most famous working wardrobe in the world had been sold with the average price of a dress in excess of $41,000. Together with the catalogue sales and profits from television syndication rights, $5.6 million was raised for AIDS and cancer charities.

LOT 1

White sari-inspired chiffon dress trimmed with pearlized sequins and beads.
Designer: Gina Fratini for Hartnell
Price raised: $85,000

LOT 2

Black silk-crepe cocktail dress with asymmetric ruched bodice and side sash. Worn at the Serpentine Gallery, London in 1993 (see pages 152, 153 and 155).
Designer: Christina Stambolian (off-the-peg)
Price raised: $74,000

LOT 3

Grey silk halterneck dress embroidered in a scroll pattern with glass beads. Worn at the Serpentine Gallery, London in 1995
Designer: Catherine Walker
Price raised: $77,300

LOT 4

Black cocktail dress with white satin collars and cuffs. Embroidered with black sequins and trimmed with a large black bow.
Designer: Bellville Sassoon, Lorcan Mullany
Price raised: $43,700

LOT 5

Fuchsia-pink, sari-style, chiffon ball dress with purple sash forming shoulder strap and trailing stole, worn on an official visit to Thailand (see pages 98 and 99).
Designer: Catherine Walker
Price raised: $48,300

LOT 6

Pale-blue chiffon ball dress with matching stole inspired by Grace Kelly. Worn at the Cannes Film Festival in 1987 and the opening of Miss Saigon in 1989 (see page 65).
Designer: Catherine Walker
Price raised: $70,700

LOT 7

White silk-chiffon evening dress decorated with pink glass beads, simulated pearls and silver and pearlized sequins and belted with white satin cord.
Designer: Zandra Rhodes
Price raised: $41,400

LOT 8

A bois de rose strapless taffeta evening dress decorated with blue flowers. Worn on a state visit to Melbourne in 1988 (see pages 96 and 97).
Designer: Catherine Walker
Price raised: $50,600

LOT 9

Pink chiffon evening dress with the bodice embroidered in a paisley style in simulated pearls. Worn for a Snowdon shoot and in Pakistan in 1991 (see pages 132, 133 and 134).
Designer: Catherine Walker
Price raised: $51,750

LOT 10

Black silk-velvet cocktail dress with black and ivory trimmed neckline, cuffs and hem.
Designer: Catherine Walker
Price raised: $34,500

Lot 6 The ice-blue chiffon dress and stole, inspired by Grace Kelly and worn at the Cannes Film Festival, was bought by Kate McEnroe, president of American Movie Classics and the Romance Channel. A strategic buyer, she also bought Diana's favourite dress – lot 80, the satin ballgown and bolero embroidered in Paris, by Victor Edelstein and lot 39, the Catherine Walker black silk dress with diamanté embroidery.

LOT 11

Midnight-blue cocktail dress with white satin collar and cuffs, blue enamel and paste buttons and a diamant buckle on a belt at the waist.
Designer: Catherine Walker
Price raised: $66,300

LOT 12

Dinner dress with black Hussar-style bodice and pleated red silk-crêpe skirt trimmed with soutache braid and rouleaux at the waist to give it a military feel.
Designer: Catherine Walker
Price raised: $36,800

LOT 14

Red chiffon dress embroidered in a tartan design in silver lamé. Worn to the premiere of *Hot Shots* in 1991.
Designer: Bruce Oldfield
Price raised: $34,500

Lot 3 This grey silk cocktail dress embroidered with glass beads was bought by Jacqueline Nims for the Fashion Café.

Lot 14 One of five Bruce
Oldfield dresses sold in
the auction, Diana wore this
spangled pepper-red chiffon
dress to a premiere of the
movie *Hot Shots*.

LOT 19

Pink evening dress. Bodice and matching
bolero embroidered with sequins, gold glass
beads and gold braid to echo Mughal motifs.
Worn during her tour of India in 1992 (see
pages 120 and 121).
Designer: Catherine Walker
Price raised: $61,900

LOT 20

One-shoulder white columnar dress
embroidered all over with translucent glass
beads and crystals. Worn in Japan and to film
premieres including *Octopussy* in 1983 (see
pages 66 and 67).
Designer: Hachi
Price raised: $75,100

LOT 21

Royal-blue satin cocktail dress with padded
off-the-shoulder collar and hem and
decorated with rectangular paste buttons.
Designer: Victor Edelstein
Price raised: $29,900

LOT 22

Ballerina-length dress with black bodice
embroidered with blue stars. The drop-
waisted skirt is a double-layer of royal blue
organza. Worn in Florence in 1985 (see
pages 80 and 81).
Designer: Jacques Azagury
Price raised: $26,450

LOT 23

Pale-blue tulle evening dress embroidered
overall with pearlized sequins and trimmed
with a pale pink sash.
Designer: Emanuel
Price raised: $27,600

LOT 24

Ivory satin thirties-style evening dress with a
silk lace overjacket. Worn at a State Banquet
at Buckingham Palace for President
Mubarak of Egypt.
Designer: Bruce Oldfield
Price raised: $29,900

LOT 25

Burgundy velvet ball dress with gathered
bodice and skirt and long sleeves with
rouleaux down the outside arm.
Designer: Catherine Walker
Price raised: $39,100

LOT 26

White silk and organza ball dress decorated
with gilt beads, gold paillettes and simulated
pearls.
Designer: Emanuel
Price raised: $25,300

LOT 27

Cream silk chiffon evening dress with
embroidered hourglass shaped bodice and
Tudor-style neckline. Worn in 1990 at a
reception at Buckingham Palace.
Designer: Catherine Walker
Price raised: $51,750

LOT 15

Green velvet thirties-style dinner dress
trimmed with three buttons on the back and
each cuff.
Designer: Victor Edelstein
Price raised: $66,300

LOT 16

White silk-crêpe dinner dress with knotted
detail bodice creating a cap sleeve effect.
Ordered for a State Banquet for the King
and Queen of Malaya in 1993.
Designer: Catherine Walker
Price raised: $52,900

LOT 17

Dinner dress with green and cream horizontally
striped bodice and green skirt, split to the
knee. Worn to the premiere of *Accidental Hero*
in 1993 (see pages 160 and 161).
Designer: Catherine Walker
Price raised: $34,500

LOT 18

Pale-blue chiffon and lace evening dress with
demi train and two trailing ties. Worn on an
official visit to the Cameroons in 1989.
Designer: Catherine Walker
Price raised: $36,800

Lot 18: Pale blue chiffon and
sequinned lace dress by
Catherine Walker, originally
made with long sleeves for the
Princess to wear in Muslim
Qatar in 1986. Later, she had it
made into this strapless dress.

Lot 23 Sequinned tulle ball dress from Diana's early 'fairy princess' period, by the designers of her wedding dress, David and Elizabeth Emanuel. The two dresses by these designers in the auction sold for a total of $52,900.

LOT 32

Burgundy, silk-velvet columnar dress decorated with shimmering pink pearls at the neckline and split to the knee at the back. Worn at Sandringham and Balmoral.
Designer: Catherine Walker
Price raised: $29,900

LOT 33

Evening dress with black velvet bodice piped in red and a full skirt of green, black and red silk in a plaid design. First worn for a dance at Balmoral.
Designer: Catherine Walker
Price raised: $46,000

LOT 34

Emerald-green satin ball dress with a Victorian-style bustle and a full skirt. Worn in an official portrait by the late Terence Donovan.
Designer: Victor Edelstein
Price raised: $27,600

LOT 35

Red lace cocktail dress with cap sleeves and a halterneck. Worn during an official visit to Argentina (see pages 172 and 173).
Designer: Catherine Walker
Price raised: $25,300

LOT 36

Black velvet dinner dress with white satin collar.
Designer: Catherine Walker
Price raised: $28,750

LOT 37

Black velvet evening dress with a V-neck and a V at the back with a slightly gathered skirt. Worn at the Gala performance of *Les Misérables* in 1985.
Designer: Bruce Oldfield
Price raised: $36,800

LOT 38

Double-breasted black and white cocktail dress with square neckline and long sleeves.
Designer: Catherine Walker
Price raised: $36,800

LOT 39

Black silk-crêpe evening dress. Empire-style bodice embroidered with diamanté paste. Worn on an official visit to India in 1992 (see pages 114, 142 and 143).
Designer: Catherine Walker
Price raised: $42,550

LOT 40

Royal-blue evening dress with velvet bodice and duchesse satin cummerbund and skirt.
Designer: Catherine Walker
Price raised: $28,750

LOT 41

Grey silk sarong-style evening dress embroidered with simulated pearls.
Designer: Catherine Walker
Price raised: $29,900

Lot 26 This was the second time this dress had been sold in a charity auction. Diana bought it at an action in aid of the Red Cross. Its second buyer was a housewife from Virginia.

LOT 28

Midnight-blue silk-tulle, strapless dress lined with purple silk and decorated with daimant stars. First worn at a dinner given by King Constantine of the Hellenes at Claridges in 1986 (see page 73).
Designer: Murray Arbeid
Price raised: $48,300

LOT 29

Midnight-blue silk-crêpe halterneck dress. Worn at the Serpentine Gallery, London in 1993 (see page 159).
Designer: Victor Edelstein
Price raised: $70,700

LOT 30

Fuchsia-pink silk off-the-shoulder evening dress. Worn at the Mansion House for a banquet in aid of Help the Hospice (see page 125).
Designer: Victor Edelstein
Price raised: $36,800

LOT 31

Bottle-green velvet double-breasted evening dress, reminiscent of a smoking jacket.
Designer: Catherine Walker
Price raised: $24,150

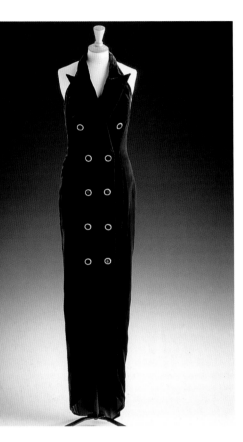

Lot 31 Dark green velvet dress by Catherine Walker, in the style of a smoking jacket, ordered for formal dinners at Balmoral, Sandringham and Windsor. Diana is said to have had a matching dinner jacket made for Charles: whether he ever wore it remains unknown.

LOT 42

Emerald-green, silk-georgette dance dress with a crossover bodice. Worn to an official banquet at The Dorchester Hotel in London in 1982.
Designer: Catherine Walker
Price raised: $24,150

LOT 43

Dinner dress with a straight black silk skirt and asymmetrical bodice decorated with white ribbon lace. Worn on the royal visit to Pakistan in 1992.
Designer: Catherine Walker
Price raised: $29,900

LOT 44

Ball dress with black velvet strapless bodice and red taffeta skirt in the flamenco style. Originally worn to a film premiere and later on an official tour of Spain (see pages 88 and 89).
Designer: Murray Arbeid
Price raised: $25,300

LOT 45

Asymmetric silk-taffeta dress printed with red roses. Worn on an official visit to Paris in 1988 (see page 102).
Designer: Catherine Walker
Price raised: $27,600

LOT 46

Ivory satin dinner dress with a bodice decorated with simulated pink pearls, glass beads and sequins. Only ever worn for private state occasions at Buckingham Palace (see pages 122 and 123).
Designer: Catherine Walker
Price raised: $25,300

LOT 47

Pink chiffon dress decorated with pearl necklaces, lace and beads. Worn on an official visit to Japan in 1986 (see page 88).
Designer: Zandra Rhodes
Price raised: $27,600

LOT 48

White silk-crêpe strapless dress decorated with horizontal bands of black velvet.
Designer: Catherine Walker
Price raised: $25,300

LOT 49

Evening dress with a black velvet bodice and bolero jacket and contrasting white taffeta skirt.
Designer: Murray Arbeid
Price raised: $24,150

LOT 50

V-necked dress decorated all over with deep-green sequins and loosely ruched at the front. Worn on an official visit to Vienna in 1986 (see pages 108 and 109).
Designer: Catherine Walker
Price raised: $24,150

LOT 51

Blue silk-crêpe dinner dress decorated at the neckline with blue satin rouleaux. Worn to the CFDA awards in New York in 1996 (see page 162).
Designer: Catherine Walker
Price raised: $36,800

LOT 52

Lilac dress with bodice and bolero jacket embroidered with violet and roses and decorated with beads. Worn on the official tour of Korea in 1992 (see pages 144 and 145).
Designer: Catherine Walker
Price raised: 51,750

LOT 53

White lace dress in the style of a double-breasted coat. Decorated with pale-blue silk flowers and white sequins. Worn on the official tour of Paris in 1988 (see pages 100 and 101).
Designer: Catherine Walker
Price raised: $27,600

LOT 54

Cream silk dinner dress with a wide leather belt trimmed with a large medallion of paste and simulated pearls. First worn to a reception in London in 1982 and again on a trip to Nepal in 1993 (see page 146).
Designer: Catherine Walker
Price raised: $34,500

Lot 3 Velvet and plaid silk dress, by Catherine Walker, ordered by Diana for Scottish dancing at Balmoral - a royal tradition kept up by the Queen. It is one of the many tartan outfits that Diana wore north of the border.

Lot 34 Victor Edelstein designed this emerald satin ballgown on Victorian lines, with a bustle and an off-the-shoulder neckline. Diana wore it for one of her official portraits, with the tiara given her by the Queen.

LOT 55

Black velvet Victorian-style dress decorated with jet beads and trimmed at the neckline and cuffs with Honiton lace.
Designer: Catherine Walker
Price raised: $24,150

LOT 56

Magenta silk Goya-esqe dress overlaid with black lace. Worn on an official visit to Germany in 1987 (see page 91).
Designer: Victor Edelstein
Price raised: $25,300

LOT 57

Pink satin dinner dress with white raw silk collar and cuffs in a nautical style. Worn on an official visit to Germany in 1987 (see page 87).
Designer: Catherine Walker
Price raised: $28,750

Lot 38: As well as the extravagant ball dresses, the sale also featured many of Diana's simple but sophisticated cocktail dresses that she had worn to attend events since her separation from Charles.

LOT 58

Asymmetric navy-blue silk evening dress trimmed in a nautical style with three rows of gold braid at the neckline and cuff.
Designer: Catherine Walker
Price raised: $23,000

LOT 59

Strapless dress of cream silk organza printed with pink, blue and yellow roses.
Designer: Catherine Walker
Price raised: $24,150

LOT 60

Evening dress with black faille bodice and jade silk-crepe skirt decorated with a fringed sash.
Designer: Catherine Walker
Price raised: $24,150

LOT 61

Aubergine silk-velvet ball dress with a tulip-shaped skirt, decorated with three paste buttons.
Designer: Victor Edelstein
Price raised: $24,150

LOT 62

Halterneck dress with a pale-yellow silk bodice and blue wraparound skirt. Worn at the premiere of *Far and Away* in 1992.
Designer: Catherine Walker
Price raised: $33,350

Lot 42 Grass-green silk georgette dress by Catherine Walker, worn by Diana to an official banquet at the Dorchester Hotel in London in 1982. She wore it with her emeralds, a green satin purse and high green satin shoes with jewelled buttons on the toes.

205

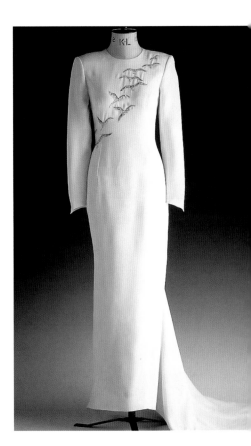

Lot 47 Fragile pink silk dress finished with delicate beading by Zandra Rhodes. Worn by Diana to a state banquet in Kyoto where she famously used her chopsticks the wrong way round.

LOT 63

Burgundy velvet dinner dress with a tailcoat embroidered in gold thread with flowers and leaves. Worn to the premiere of *Steel Magnolias* in 1990.
Designer: Catherine Walker
Price raised: $26,450

LOT 64

Cream silk dinner dress embroidered with gold and silver sequinned falcons. Worn on a state visit to Saudi Arabia (see page 94).
Designer: Catherine Walker
Price raised: $35,650

LOT 65

Ivory silk-crêpe evening dress decorated with pink sequins. Worn on an official visit to Brazil in 1991 (see page 141).
Designer: Catherine Walker
Price raised: $26,450

LOT 66

Black halterneck dress trimmed at the neckline and one hip with black bugle beads. Worn at Versailles in 1994 (see page 158).
Designer: Catherine Walker
Price raised: $57,500

LOT 67

Scarlet silk dress with a long bodice embroidered with beads. Worn on an official visit to Saudi Arabia.
Designer: Bruce Oldfield
Price raised: $23,000

Lot 64 One of the dresses from Diana's diplomatic wardrobe for her visit to Saudi Arabia, by Catherine Walker. The cream silk dress was decorously cut and decorated with sequinned falcons, as a compliment to her hosts.

LOT 68

Royal-blue Fortuny-style dress decorated with bugle beads at the neckline and waist. Worn on a state visit to Japan in 1986 (see pages 104 and 105).
Designer: Yuki
Price raised: $25,300

LOT 69

White silk-chiffon halterneck dress printed with purple tulips and green leaves. Worn on an official visit to Nigeria in 1989 (see page 115).
Designer: Catherine Walker
Price raised: $25,300

LOT 70

Pale blue-grey chiffon dress with a high-cut bodice embroidered with rows of simulated pearls, glass beads and paste. Worn to a reception at Spencer House in 1992.
Designer: Catherine Walker
Price raised: $36,800

Lot 54 The jewellery maker who bought this dress by Catherine Walker stripped the pearl beads from the bodice to sell as 'Diana earrings' in the States.

LOT 71

Long dinner dress with a cream silk bodice and salmon-pink silk skirt. Worn at the first night of *Swan Lake* at the London Coliseum (see page 116).
Designer: Catherine Walker
Price raised: $25,300

LOT 72

Salmon-pink silk dinner dress with a long tunic-style bodice embroidered with simulated pearls and paste. Worn to a Gala Evening for the English National Ballet in 1993.
Designer: Catherine Walker
Price raised: $21,850

LOT 73

Purple crushed-velvet dress with a cowl collar and train attached at the hip. Worn on an official visit to Portugal in 1987 (see page 83).
Designer: Bruce Oldfield
Price raised: $26,450
Buyer: Donna Coffin, Chicago, USA

LOT 74

Burgundy velvet long-sleeved dinner dress with a low V-back. Worn to the premiere of *Back to the Future* in 1985 (see page 69).
Designer: Catherine Walker
Price raised: $26,450

LOT 75

Black silk-velvet dress cut as a pastiche of a tailcoat and edged with black ribbed silk. Worn to the premiere of *Dangerous Liaisons* in 1989 (see pages 118 and 119).
Designer: Victor Edelstein
Price raised: $31,050

LOT 76

Strapless ball dress with black silk-velvet bodice and deep burgundy and black silk skirt.
Designer: Catherine Walker
Price raised: $24,150

LOT 77

Black evening dress with shoulder straps embroidered with gold sequins, gold bugle beads and paste. Worn on an official visit to Canada in 1991.
Designer: Bellville Sassoon and Lorcan Mullany
Catherine Walker:
Price raised: $23,000

LOT 78

White silk-crêpe sheath dress and matching high-collared jacket embroidered all over with simulated pearls and white sequins, dubbed the 'Elvis' dress by Diana (see pages 130 and 131).
Designer: Catherine Walker
Price raised: $151,000

Lot 72 Even the dress that raised the lowest price earned $21,850 for Diana's favourite charities.

Lot 73 This regal dress by Bruce Oldfield, worn by Diana on an official visit to Portugal, was bought at auction by Donna Coffin, a mother of three from Chicago, Illinois.

LOT 79

Blue silk-velvet dinner dress with off-the-shoulder straps and a slight bustle. Worn at the White House on the famous occasion when Diana danced with John Travolta (see page 85).
Designer: Victor Edelstein
Price raised: $222,500

LOT 80

Oyster duchesse-satin dress with a bodice and bolero embroidered by Hurel with flowers and birds in simulated pearls, paste and beads. Worn at a banquet at the Elysée Palace in 1988 and for a photographic shoot by Terence Donovan (see pages 106 and 107).
Designer: Victor Edelstein
Price raised: $90,500

DRESSES

from the
Collection of Diana, Princess of Wales

A charity sale conducted by Christie's
on a not-for-profit basis

CHRISTIE'S

DESIGNERS

MURRAY ARBEID

Arbeid began his career in 1
apprentice to Michael Shera
he set up on his own, openi
business in 1954. In the late
he acted as a consultant to
Norman Hartnell. He is nov
retired.

Over the years Diana had
number of evening dresses k
Arbeid including a striking
diamant-starred blue dress tl
wore to a number of occasic
the mid-eighties (see page 7

JACQUES AZAGURY

Azagury was trained at St.
Martin's School of Art in L
and at his final-year show w
hailed as one of the most
promising new designers. H
first collection was bought l
Browns and he went on to
his designs all over the worl
He opened his flagship stor
Knightsbridge, London in
1987.

Azagury was a great
favourite of Diana's. His fir:
dress for her was a twenties
style ballgown worn in the
mid-eighties. He went on t
design some of her most da
and sexy dresses during the
few years of her life, includ
the black evening dress she
the night her Panorama
interview was broadcast (se
pages
178 and 179).

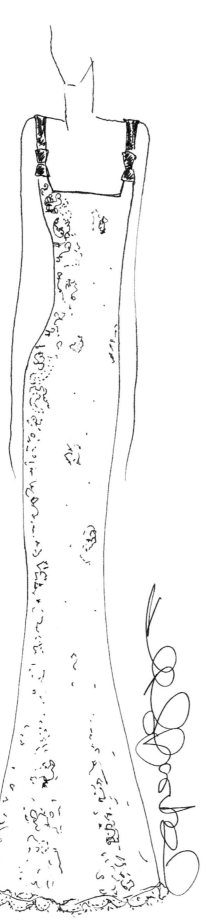

CAROLINE CHARLES

Charles was trained at the Swindon School of Art before beginning
work for Mary Quant. In 1963 she set up on her own and soon
became known as one of the ëswinging' sixties set, designing for
celebrities like Cilla Black, Ringo Starr and Mick Jagger. Thirty years
later her clothes are still worn all over the world and she has shops in
London's Bond Street and Beauchamp Place.

Charles's clothes are distinctive for their use of luxury fabrics and
the clothes she made for the newly married Princess of Wales were
no exception, a tartan dress (see page 55) and luxuriant oatmeal coat
(see page 47) are two of her most memorable creations.

JASPER CONRAN

Conran trained at the Parsons School of Art and Design in New
York before returning to his birthplace, London, to establish
himself as a fashion designer. He started his ready-to-wear label
in 1978 and amongst his accolades was awarded the British
Council Fashion Designer of the Year Award (1986–87).

Conran was a close confidante of Diana's and she had hoped
he would fill the role as her exclusive designer for some of the
royal tours. Although Conran turned down the job, he continued
to be a great source of many of the clothes the Princess wore in
private including leather jackets and jeans.

VICTOR EDELSTEIN

Born in London, Edelstein began as a trainee designer at Alexon in
1962. He went on to work for Biba, Salvador and Dior before
setting up on his own in 1978. As well as being an established
couturier he also designed for the theatre and ballet. He now
prefers to paint than design clothes and has retired to Italy (chk) to
pursue this interest.

Edelstein designed some of Diana's most stunning evening wear
including the fuchsia-pink dress that she wore so many times in
the early nineties (see page 125) and the ink-blue velvet gown
that she was wearing when she danced with John Travolta in
Washington (see page 85).

ELIZABETH AND DAVID EMANUEL

The Emanuels met in 1976 and were the first married couple to be accepted by the Royal College of Art to study for a Masters degree in Fashion. On leaving they opened their first salon in Brook Street and followed this with the Emanuel Shop in London's prestigious Beauchamp Place in 1987. The couple split in 1990 but both continue to design under their own names with Elizabeth working from the Brook Street salon.

The Emanuels are best known as the designers of Diana's fairy-tale wedding dress in 1981 (see pages 38–9, 40 and 41). Chosen by Diana herself, after she had worn one of their blouses for a Vogue sitting, she continued to wear their designs into the eighties.

GINA FRATINI

Born in Japan, Fratini was educated in Britain and Canada before becoming a student of the Royal College of Art in London. After graduating she worked as a costume and set designer for a dance troupe and continued to work freelance for eleven years before establishing Gina Fratini Limited in 1964.

Fratini designed some of Diana's most ëroyal' dresses including a white chiffon evening dress that Diana wore for a Patrick Demarchelier sitting and the cream satin dress that she was much photographed in on her tour of New Zealand in 1983 (see page 49).

JOHN GALLIANO

Galliano graduated from St Martin's School of Art in London in 1984 to unprecedented acclaim and produced his first signature collection the following year. He has received high praise for every collection since and has been winner of the British Designer of the Year award three times. In 1995 he was appointed designer for the House of Givenchy and in late 1996 he became Design Director for the House of Dior.

Soon after his move to Dior the Princess of Wales was first seen in a Galliano creation. The navy blue slip dress provoked much comment when she wore it in New York in December 1996 (see page 163).

MARGARET HOWELL

Howell began designing accessories in the late sixties before moving onto men's then women's clothing in the mid-seventies. She opened her first shop in London in 1980 and today has shops and concessions in Europe, America and especially Japan. In 1995 she showed her first collection in London Fashion Week.

Howell has expressed an enjoyment in grouping items together to make a statement and it was an outfit of this type – a white tuxedo with black bow tie – with which the Princess of Wales provoked much press attention at a Genesis concert in March 1984 (see page 77).

ROLAND KLEIN

Born in France and educated at the famous …cole de la Chambre Syndicale in Paris, Klein began his work in the fashion houses of Dior and Patou before moving to London in the late sixties. Here he set up his own boutique in Chelsea and established his own label. Today his clothes are available throughout the UK, USA and Japan.

Known for his understated chic, Klein designed clothes for Diana throughout her time in the public eye including one of her favourite outfits – frequently seen at polo matches and informal occasions – a trompe l'oeil jumper decorated with rhinestones (see page 34).

BRUCE OLDFIELD

Oldfield trained at St Martin's School of Art in the early seventies and gained his first commission upon leaving. This was shortly followed by his first show in the US in 1973. Since then he has been a constant player in the international fashion scene, known for both his couture and his ready-to-wear collections.

Oldfield and Diana had a strong relationship due to their interest in charitable causes. He was a particularly strong influence in the mid-eighties when he encouraged Diana to wear more extravagant and daring styles, most notably the gold lam dress which earned her the headline ëDynasty Di' (see page 72).

RIFAT OZBEK

Ozbek was born in Istanbul and came to England to ;
architecture but later changed direction to fashon and
studied at St Martin's School of Art. He formed his o'
company in 1984 and in 1987 launched his Future O
diffusion line. His New Age collection, all in white, ir
was a major turning point and as a result he received
Glamour Award from the British Fashion industry. In
he staged his debut fashion show having previously
presented his shows on video.

Diana discovered Ozbek's name in a magazine and
went to him at the time of the launch of his diffusion
line for some revealing dresses that were saved for
private occasions.

ZANDRA RHODES

Rhodes was
introduced to the
world of fashion by
her mother who
worked as a fitter in a Paris fashion
house. She was trained at the Royal
College of Art and opened her first
shop on the Fulham Road, London
in 1969. She was one of a number
of London designers in the
forefront of the international
fashion scene in the seventies and
has retained a cult following of
devotees.

Rhodes' designs are bold and
distinctive, often inspired by her multi-
cultural interests making her a perfect
designer for Diana as can be seen in the
unusual pink dress that the Princess
wore on an official visit to Japan in 1986
(see pages 88 and 204).

DAVID SASSOON

Sassoon trained at the Royal
College of Art before setting
up Bellville Sassoon with
Belinda (chk) Bellville
thirty five years ago. He
now controls the company
and was joined by Lorcan
Mullany in 1987. Both
designers now work under
their joint name, selling their
clothes through many prestigious
stores worldwide.

Diana was first introduced to
Bellville Sassoon by her mother who
had often worn their clothes. The first
outfit she asked them to design was her
going-away outfit (see pages 36 and 37)
and they were to design winter coats,
maternity wear and evening wear for her
throughout her life.

CHRISTINA STAMBOLIAN

Trained in her native Greece Stambolian came
to London in 1970 to work as a designer. Since
1978 she has produced an eighty-piece
collection for each season and has developed a
particular interest in the fabrics of the far east.
Today she works as a head designer for a well
known London company and continues to make
private commissions.

Stambolian is best known as the designer of the
ëvengeance dress' that Diana wore to the Serpentine
Gallery on the night Charles's Panorama interview
was broadcast in 1992 (see pages 152,153 and 155).

TOMASZ STARZEWSKI

Starzewski was trained at St Martin's School of Art and had his first boutique in the Old Brompton Road. In only seven years he has established himself as one of the most popular society dressers and has received many nominations for the Couture and Glamour categories of the British Fashion awards.

Starzewski claims his clothes are for confident women who are not afraid to make an entrance and so it not surprising that he became one of Diana's chosen designers in the years after her separation from Charles. He designed many striking suits for functions and tours including a navy-and-white outfit worn on the fiftieth anniversary of VJ day (see page 167).

VALENTINO

Born in northern Italy, Valentino moved to Paris in the fifties where, after attending design classes, he was apprenticed by Jean Dess s and Guy Laroche. He returned to Italy and set up his atelier in the early sixties. He received considerable acclaim during the sixties, dressing Hollywood stars and international royalty. In many ways he set the precedent for those who came after him, launching a ready-to-wear range alongside his couture and signing merchandising agreements to sue his name. He has continued to be a huge name in international fashion boasting many of the world's most beautiful women as his clients.

Once released of her obligation to dress in British-designed clothes, Diana was free to wear outfits by Valentino including the wine-coloured velvet dress she wore to a Hong Kong Gala at the Barbican (see pages 156 and 157).

JAN VANVELDEN

The Dutchman Vanvelden trained as a dress designer in Amsterdam and London, where he now lives. He came to England in 1962 and in 1964 he set up his own company, *Jan Vanvelden* which he ran for twenty-five years. He now acts as a consultant, working closely with Tomasz Starzewski.

Vanvelden worked closely with Diana in the eighties, and is known for the range of maternity wear that he designed for her. He was introduced to the Princess by Vogue's Anna Harvey and Beatrice Miller and was commissioned to design outfits for her for several years after that.

GIANNI VERSACE

Versace was born in Calabria, Italy where he learnt dress making from his mother. In 1972 he moved to Milan to work as a fashion designer and in 1975 presented his first collection for Complice. His first own-name collection was in 1978 and from then on he became an international celebrity designing outrageous outfits for the likes of Elton John and Madonna.

Although renowned for his opulent designs, Versace was a strong influence in creating Diana's pared down minimal style in the later years of her life, designing some of her most memorable outfits including the dress on the cover of this book.

AMANDA WAKELEY

Wakeley has been working in fashion since 1984 and founded her company in 1990. Her clothes are sold throughout the world and she has two retail outlets in London. She is the only designer to have won the Glamour Award in the British Fashion Awards three times, most recently in 1996.

Wakeley is best known for her simple but stylish separates and was a great influence on Diana as she developed her working wardrobe in the early nineties providing her with many of her most feminine suits including the one she wore when she resigned from public life (see page 147).

CATHERINE WALKER

Born and educated in France, Walker set up her couture house The Chelsea Design Company Limited in 1978. During her career she has received two Designer of the Year Awards, the first, the British Couture Award in 1991 and the Glamour Award the following year.

Walker was the most prolific of Diana's designers, often creating a complete wardrobe for foreign tours. She designed by far the majority of Diana's evening wear and this was reflected in the enormous number of her dresses that were sold in the Christie's auction in 1997.

YUKI

Born in Japan, Yuki was educated in Chicago and London, graduating from the London College of Fashion in 1966. His first job was a pattern cutter before going on to work for Michael of Carlos Place, Norman Hartnell and Pierre Cardin. He launched his first own-name collection at Harvey Nicholls in 1972. He now licenses under his Japanese name Gnyuki Torimaru and has a shop of the same name in Belgravia, London.

Diana was always keen to wear dresses by native designers when she went on foreign tours and in 1986 it was suggested to her that she approach Yuki for an outfit for her Japanese tour (see pages 104 and 105).

RONIT ZILKHA

Zilkha established her ready-to-wear label in 1991 and has built up a loyal following of women looking for classic clothes with an edge. Her clothes range from simple tailoring to glamorous evening wear. She now has four stores in London, concessions elsewhere in Britain and a thriving export business including Europe and the Far East.

Zilkha's classic tailored suits became a favourite of Diana's during the last few years of her life and she could often be seen wearing them at charity events or for informal meetings with friends.

SHOEMAKERS

MANOLO BLAHNIK

Blahnik claims to have learnt his skills from his mother who made shoes for the family and still corrects his sketches today. His first job in fashion was in Paris in 1968 where he worked as a shop assistant before moving to London and began to design shoes in a tiny shop called Zapanta. Today his shoes are worn by the world's richest women many of whom own vast collections of his work. Blahnik's shoes have been described as giving women legs and it was his feminine, sexy styles which attracted Diana. She had many different colours of her favourite design (see page 00).

JIMMY CHOO

Choo lost count of the shoes he made for Diana. After the separation she could frequently be seen in his delicate high-heeled shoes – a style that she could not wear when she was accompanying her husband for fear of towering over him – while for informal occasions she favoured his classic pump.

MILLINERS

JOHN BOYD

Boyd has been making hats for over fifty years. Originally from Edinburgh he has had a number of shops in west London and is currently based in Beauchamp Place.

Boyd had been a favourite of the royals for many years – he has designed Princess Anne's hats since she was sixteen – and so was a natural choice for Diana when she first joined the royal family. He made the famous tricorn hat that she wore with her going-away outfit (see page 36). The style became known as the ëLady Di' shape and was copied worldwide.

FREDERICK FOX

Fox was brought up on a farm in New South Wales and realising his talent in millinery moved to London via Paris in the fifties. He established himself in Britain and in 1974 was issued a royal warrant by the Queen. The loyalty he evokes from one generation to the next has guaranteed that he has remained in the very forefront of hat design ever since.

Fox was a great influence on Diana during the mid-eighties when she began experimenting with wider brims. She was seen wearing his flying-saucer shaped hats at Ascot in 1985 (see page 62) and on the official royal tour of Italy in the same year.

STEPHEN JONES

Jones opened his first salon in a store in 1980. He has gone on to design hats for some of the most renowned fashion designers including Thierry Mugler and Jean Paul Gaultier. He has his two diffusion lines, Miss Jones and Jonesboy and is also a consultant for Shiseido cosmetics.

Jones's work is esoteric and in the early eighties his work had appeared in many pop videos. As Diana experimented with less traditional royal clothes in the mid-eighties she often turned to Jones for her hats, wishing to branch out from the traditional royal milliners.

GRAHAM SMITH

British milliner Graham Smith studied at Bromley College of Art and the Royal College of Art, London. He began his career as cheif milliner at Lanvin in Paris, returning to England to become Design Director of Kangol. In 1998 he became millinery consultant to British Home Stores in the UK, producing an exclusive range of hats in selected stores.

His work has been featured in numerous leading publications in the United Kingdom as well as being seen on major television and radio programmes on many occasions. His model lines are available to a wide range and notable circle of private customers from his Crawford Street premises.

PHILIP SOMERVILLE

Somerville moved to London from New Zealand in the early sixties. He worked as Otto Lucas's PA before his death after which Somerville set up his own work room just off Bond Street. Here began his flourishing wholesale business which continues today from new premises on Chiltern Street. He now designs hat for the Queen and was recently given a Royal Warrant. Somerville's striking style is widely recognized and he was influential in changing the direction of the Princess's hats over the eleven years he worked for her, most often creating brightly coloured wide-brimmed hats to coordinate with outfits by her favourite designers such as Catherine Walker (see page 82).

Index

SOURCES

Diana: Her True Story – In Her Own Words, Andrew Morton, Michael O'Mara Books, 1997
The Royal Jewels, Suzy Menkes, Grafton Books, 1985
Requiem: Diana Princess of Wales 1961-1997, edited by Brian MacArthur, Pavilion, 1997
Christie's Catalogue - Dresses from the Collection of Diana, Princess of Wales, 1997

PICTURE CREDITS

The photographs listed below are protected by copyright.
All still-lifes and fabric details of the dresses are by Stephen Hayward.
All reportage photographs other than those specified below are © Anwar Hussein.

Alpha: 70, 100 *top*, 117, 162 *top*, 187, 192.
Aurelia PR: 174.
Camera Press: 16, 19, 20-21, 27, 38-39, 65, 84, 87, 100 *bottom*, 106, 109, 110, 120, 122-123, 128, 131, 139, 142 *top*, 167, 175.
Patrick Demarchelier: 6, 135.
Terence Donovan: 65, 87, 106, 131.
Jayne Fincher/Photographers International: 111, 113, 136-137.
Sasha Gusov: 198-199, 208-209.
Stephen Hayward/Camera Press: 66 *bottom*, 73 *bottom*, 81, 89, 94, 96 *top*, 97, 98, 101, 102 bottom, 104, 105 *bottom*, 107, 108, 119, 121, 122 *left*, 130, 132, 134, 142-143, 144, 152, 160, 162 *bottom*, 173, 200-207.
Patrick Lichfield: 38-39.
PA News: 189.
Rex Features: 80 *top*, 85, 116, 124, 129, 140, 155, 197.
Snowdon: 19, 27, 120, 122-123, 128.
John Swannell: 20-21.
Sygma: 194-195.
UK Press: 150, 164, 180, 185, 186, 193, 219 *top right*, 219 *bottom right*.

The publishers would like to thank the following for kindly supplying the sketches of their designs and the photographs on pages 210-215:

Azagury, Manolo Blahnik, John Boyd, Jasper Conran, the Emanuels, John Galliano, Margaret Howell, Roland Klein, Rifat Ozbek, Zandra Rhodes, David Sassoon, Philip Somerville, Christina Stambolian, Tomasz Starzewski, Valentino, Versace, Amanda Wakeley, Yuki, Ronit Zilkha.